Gerd Ludwig

300 Questions About Cats

- ➤ Compact Information from A to Z
- ➤ Practical Advice for Every Situation

Contents

Healthy Diet ?

Contents

Health and Grooming

■ Anatomy and the Senses ?

Contents

Language and Behavior ?

Acquisition, the Law, and Equipment

Anyone who decides to live with a cat
is entering into a relationship that
can last for fifteen years and longer.
In this section, you'll find answers to
all the important questions that you
should ask when starting out with
your new housemate.

1. **Accessories: The range of cat accessories is almost too vast to comprehend. What makes the most sense?**

The basic equipment in a cat's home includes a cat basket or bed, food and water bowls, a litter box, a scratching post or scratch board, cat grass, a medicine chest, and a pet carrier (see Equipment and Accessories, page 22). With the right accessories, it is easier to groom the cat and keep it healthy. Useful accessories also help the cat feel contented in its home and prevent boredom when it is alone.

➤ Grooming accessories: Natural bristles and nylon or Perlon bristles reduce static electricity in your pet's coat, and the rounded teeth of metal combs guard against injury, while sturdy handles ensure that you wield the brush and comb properly. Bathe only with pet shampoo labeled as being safe for use on cats.

➤ Toys: Good cat toys improve the cat's level of physical fitness and ability to react, and they also ward off boredom. Popular choices are balls, feather toys, and squeaky mice. Toys for young cats in particular must be bite-proof.

➤ Climbing rope: Climbing ropes and cat trees expand the cat's range of mobility and are a good recommendation for smaller apartments in particular.

➤ Leash and harness: A walk on the leash is an alternative way of getting fresh air, if you can't give your cat an opportunity to go outdoors.

➤ Cat door (also with electronic lock): Indoor-outdoor cats can come and go at will.

2. **Acclimation: How do I make the cat's first few days in its new home easier for it?**

Your new cat needs time to find its way around in the new surroundings and make friends with the strange humans there. This is especially true for a frightened kitten. Tips on helping your pet adjust:

➤ A cozy place to nestle into and sleep provides security.

➤ Food and water bowls should have a designated location from the outset.

➤ Continue using the kind of food chosen by the previous owner, and adhere to the same feeding schedule.

➤ Set up the litter box in a quiet, out-of-the-way area, and show the cat where it is.

➤ A scratching post is an essential item of equipment.

➤ Avoid loud noises and commotion.

➤ Let the cat decide when it wants to be close to you and is ready for cuddling.

➤ Don't let the cat go outdoors in the first four weeks.

3. **Acclimation: Our cat is soon going to be joined in our home by a puppy. Will that cause problems?**

If the cat itself is still young, everything should go smoothly, as long as the puppy is not a lot larger than the kitten. Large breed, rambunctious puppies can harm a small kitten, so all meetings between cat and dog should be supervised. Young animals usually get along right off the bat and often forge a life-long friendship. A full-grown cat will tolerate the puppy only reluctantly at first because it sees a threat to its territory. In this case, male cats show more tolerance than the capricious females. Show your cat affection while the puppy watches. The cat will quickly realize that the puppy's presence in your home means something pleasant.

4. **Acquisition: Does it make more sense to buy a kitten or a full-grown cat?**

A kitten will come into your home at the age of 8 to 12 weeks. Although it is already a real little cat, in the first weeks it requires lots of time and attention, has to be fed up to five times a day, and should not be alone for long periods. For a single person who works, that means planning annual leave to accom-

At six weeks, the kittens test their physical fitness and abilities in wild scuffles. Often they get right down to the nitty-gritty.

modate the kitten's adjustment. A full-grown cat is already litter box-trained and presents virtually no problems where feeding is concerned. If it has already been spayed or neutered, you will save on this expense. Patience and experience with cats are called for, however, until the animal accepts its new environment and the new humans. Depending on its temperament and origin, it will be friendly or distant in dealing with children and other pets.

5. **Acquisition: Which is better for me as a novice cat owner, a male or a female?**

Female cats, or queens, are often especially fond of cuddling and usually bond more closely with a human than males, but they also place greater demands on the relationship and react ungraciously when they feel mistreated or neglected. A male cat is more imperturbable, but can also be stubborn and phlegmatic. Non-castrated toms that go outdoors regularly get into scraps with other males, which may result in more than trivial traces of combat. When in the mood for love, both queens and toms make life hard for their owner: A female in heat is loud and insistent, while a lovesick tom engages in marking and tries to run off. Only spaying or castration (see Info, page 148) stops the increases in hormone levels. Whether male or female, cats are independent personalities with individual needs, and the quality of your partnership depends on whether the cat feels happy living with you.

6. **Acquisition:** Is it essential to get papers when you purchase a purebred cat?

Absolutely, since the papers (pedigree, or family tree, as an excerpt from the breed registry) are simultaneously the identification card of a purebred cat. They are issued by the breed association to which the cat's breeder belongs. The breeder's activity is based on the guidelines for keeping and breeding a cat that are issued by the recognized breed club. The sale is accomplished by means of a contract of sale, and a reputable breeder usually also presents a certificate of health from a veterinarian for the cat. Purebred cats without papers not infrequently come from dubious breeding operations called "kitten mills." Often they are sold too early and without the vital inoculations.

7. **Acquisition:** If I want to keep two cats, what is the right combination?

Siblings from the same litter that grow up together are ideal. In this case, the combination of brother and sister is typically unproblematic. But since close kinship does not protect against unwanted offspring, you need to discuss a date for spaying/castration with the vet as early as possible. Two little toms, too, usually are bosom buddies, while queens can be somewhat more contrary as adults. If a kitten joins a mature male cat in your home, it often takes only a few days for him to recover from the initial surprise and take the little kitty under his wing. An adult female will be less tolerant and make an energetic protest. A lot of patience is necessary until the excitement dies down.

8. **Age when acquired:** Why don't some breeders let young cats go to a new home before they are twelve weeks old?

Starting with the sixth week of life, kittens become increasingly independent: They can eat solid foods, and some even begin to use the litter box like real pros. During this phase, the mother cat, too, is less and less willing to let her offspring nurse whenever they are so inclined. As a result, many cat owners think the little cats can now manage on their own and are ready to go to new homes. They may also be acting out of a belief that a young kitten bonds with its new owner more quickly and easily. In general, taking a kitten to its new home between eight and ten weeks of age is practical and causes no harm.

However, some breeders believe that letting a kitten go to a new home at this age does not do justice to its needs. They believe that up to the end of the third month, being raised by their mother is just as vital for the kittens' healthy development as having an opportunity to tussle and play with their littermates, which lays the foundation for feline social behaviors.

Many reputable cat owners and breeders do not send kittens to new homes until they are twelve weeks old, and some even wait an additional week. As a minimum, veterinarians recommend that kittens stay with their mothers until the age of eight weeks unless an earlier time is warranted in order to spare the mother or the kittens pain, suffering, or harm.

9. **Apartment: Can I keep a cat without the landlord's permission?**

The landlord or property owner can prohibit the keeping of pets in rental properties. The lease agreement or rental contract should clearly state this. If you violate the terms of the agreement, you are subjecting yourself to possible eviction. At the very least, you would certainly be required to give up the cat if you are discovered keeping one in an apartment where pets are prohibited. It is not fair to adopt a cat under such circumstances, knowing that you may not be able to keep it unless you move.

If pets are permitted, there are generally restrictions on how many you can have, usually only one or two. The lease agreeme'nt may further state that pets must be vaccinated according to state law and not allowed to roam outside freely. In addition, you may be required to pay a pet deposit or an extra monthly fee, in case your pet damages the property.

10. Breed association: What are the tasks and goals of a cat breeders' association?

The most important purpose of a breed association is to promote the keeping, breeding, and showing of purebred cats. The association develops breeding guidelines, maintains a breed registry in which all the breeding animals and litters are recorded, and issues proof of descent. Additional tasks: Placement of kittens and stud cats, cooperation with larger umbrella organizations (see Useful Addresses, page 239) in various ways, including coordinating the breed standard; putting on shows, club evenings, and seminars; and publishing magazines and specialized literature The largest cat association is the Cat Fanciers' Association (see Useful Addresses, page 239).

11. Breed standard: Why does a standard have to be followed in breeding purebred cats?

The breed standard is compiled by the breed association or the international umbrella organization to which the association belongs. In the standard, the ideal types of characteristics of a cat breed are defined. Depending on the breed organization that is responsible for the standard, the standards of individual breeds may differ from one another. At shows, the breed standard is the basis for doing the judging.

> **INFO**
>
> **Born with blue eyes**
> Only between the tenth and twelfth weeks do pigment cells build up in the eye, and then you can tell what color a kitten's eyes really will be later on. Until then, all kittens have blue eyes because the iris is almost devoid of pigment. Only after 3 or 4 months is the color of a cat's eyes fully developed.

12. Breeders: What constitutes a good breeder of purebred cats?

A reputable cat breeder belongs to a recognized breed club (see Useful Addresses, page 239). The housing and breeding regulations of the breed association are the foundation for his or her breeding practices.

➤ Family connection: The cats live in the breeder's family. He or she specializes in one or two breeds and keeps a limited number of animals.

➤ Cleanliness: The sleeping places are clean, and the food and water dishes are washed daily.

➤ Healthy and well groomed: All the cats make a healthy and alert impression.

➤ Visitors permitted: For the breeder, it is important for the future owner to visit the cat several times before the handover date and become acquainted.

➤ Heart and kidneys: The breeder sells an animal only if he or she is convinced that the buyer will be a suitable cat owner (see Tip, page 17).

➤ Preventive care: By the time of handover, the young cats have been vaccinated (basic series of shots) and wormed.

➤ Age at sale: The kittens usually do not leave the breeder until they are at least 12 weeks old.

➤ Black on white: Purebred cats are sold with a sales contract and papers (pedigree).

13. Breeding of defects: How is breeding governed to prevent defects?

In the United States, there are numerous cat-registering associations that govern the ethical breeding and showing of purebred cats. Each association sets its own standard for each breed, which may include a list of prohibited defects. For example, the standard may spell out the number of toes required on the cat's feet. If a cat has extra toes, it cannot be shown. Reputable breeders cull cats with known defects from their breeding stock. These folks are generally private, small-volume breeders who view breeding and showing cats as a serious hobby or profession.

However, there are plenty of inexperienced or unethical breeders out there who are more interested in turning a quick profit than in breeding animals to the highest and healthiest standard. That's why you should avoid acquiring an animal from dubious operations, such as backyard breeders and kitten mills. Backyard breeders are people who acquire a purebred and decide they want to produce a litter or two to make some extra money. They typically have little or no experience at breeding or showing cats and, therefore, may not readily recognize less obvious defects. Kitten mills are larger operations that churn out animals for sale in the pet retail market. These folks are generally more interested in quantity than quality. Some pet shops refuse to purchase animals from these types of suppliers, but the only way to know is to ask where a cat came from. If the retailer won't tell you, you would be wise to steer clear.

14. Bringing your pet home: What do I have to keep in mind when I bring my new cat home? ?

Two or three days in advance, check with the seller to make sure of the date and time for the handover. For

EXTRA TIP

Is a cat right for me?
➤ Can I offer it a cat-appropriate home?
➤ Do all the family members agree to have a cat?
➤ Will the cat have to stay alone for no more than five hours a day?
➤ Can I supply the necessary time and energy for care and attention?
➤ Can I also give up habits I'm fond of for the cat's sake?
➤ Can I come to terms with the fact that a cat sheds?
➤ Am I prepared to take care of the cat in case it becomes ill?
➤ Can I afford the routine costs and perhaps extra expenses as well?
➤ Can I afford to have the cat spayed or neutered?

For indoor cats, which are frequently alone, playtime with their owners is especially important.

a cat, losing its accustomed surroundings is a drastic event. This is especially true for a kitten, which is being separated from is mother and littermates. On the trip home in the car, a second person should take care of the frightened cat. Inside the box or carrier, a blanket with the familiar smell of home will provide warmth and security. Newspaper will protect the car seat, in case the cat's stomach reacts to the excitement. Don't feed the animal before getting in the car, take regular breaks if the drive is a long one, and offer the cat some water to drink.

15. **Burial: When my cat dies, I want to bury it in our yard. Is that permitted?**

Each city or county's local laws determine whether the interment of dogs, cats, cage birds, and other house pets in your own yard is permissible, provided the following restrictions are observed: Animals that have died of a reportable disease may not be buried. The burial site should not be located in a water protection area and must be at a sufficient distance from public thoroughfares and areas. The pit containing the animal cadaver should be covered with a layer of soil at least 20 inches (50 cm) deep. In many areas, a special permit is not required for the burial of a house pet in your own yard. However, burial of a house pet on public property, in a city park, for example, is categorically prohibited. The pet cemetery and pet crematorium are recommended as alternatives for all pet owners who lack an opportunity to bury their deceased house pet in a private yard or garden.

16. Care: I'm single and have a full-time job. Can I still try to keep a cat?

A cat can stay alone for several hours, but it should not be left by itself all day. The decisive factor is your regular daily routine with fixed times for feeding, playing, and cuddling with your cat. A cat-appropriate home will prevent boredom during your absence, and outdoor exercise also makes it easier to be alone. If you are away for more than five hours at a stretch every day, you should start out with two cats.

17. Cat basket: Why is the pretty wicker basket so rarely seen these days?

The wickerwork cat basket looks attractive but has serious drawbacks: Thorough cleaning (for example, in case of flea infestation) is virtually impossible, it offers little protection against cold and drafts, it is too cumbersome for easy transportation, and the door often does not close securely. For good reason, the sturdy, shock-resistant pet carrier made of plastic has taken the place of the basket as a mobile cat carrier.

18. Cat from a pet shelter: As a first-time cat owner, is a cat from a pet shelter too much for me to handle?

Shelter cats make the same demands as all other cats in a partnership with a human. Most of them become integrated into their new family without problems. However, you should know a little something about cats before you head off to the pet shelter. Of course, the staff members are happy every time a cat finds a home, but they won't release the rescued animals unless they are sure they are being placed in good hands. The counseling interview usually will quickly determine which cat suits you. All the cats are looked after by a vet, they are vaccinated, and they are regularly checked for parasites. Many animal shelters release their cats to new homes with a so-called protection contract, stating that the shelter remains the owner of the cat and can have the cat at any time. A return clause comes into effect if the new keeper unexpectedly has great problems with the cat. At the time of handover, a protective charge is collected, and it is intended to partially cover the shelter's expenses and to keep animals from falling into the hands of for-profit dealers.

19. Certificates: Does my cat need any kind of special papers or certificates to travel?

That depends on your destination and mode of travel. Travel to foreign countries, as well as domestic flights within the United States, nearly always require a valid rabies certificate. Some airlines and foreign destinations may require additional documentation. If you're traveling with your cat to a cat show, the show rules will in most instances require proof of vaccinations, and sometimes proof of a negative feline leukemia virus test. When transporting your cat in your personal vehicle to another state or locality, you are wise to carry a valid rabies certificate with you to your destination, in case a problem arises where you need proof of your cat's status.

20. Character: Can you tell what kind of cat a kitten will grow up to be?

Clear differences in character are evident as early as the sixth week. A kitten that is interested in everything going on near the birthing box, takes the initiative in going on expeditions, and stands up to its littermates will hold its ground as a full-grown cat as well and will assert its claims even in a boisterous family. A shy kitten needs lots of love and understanding; later on it is apt to keep its distance from other cats, but not infrequently it will bond very closely with its owner. It is the ideal partner for singles and senior citizens.

21. Condominium: Can the condo association prohibit the keeping of cats in a condominium?

The regulations of the owners' association govern the keeping of animals in a condominium. These regulations may contain a restriction or a prohibition. If the association regulations do not prohibit keeping animals, an owner generally is entitled to keep up to two cats. Some restrictions may apply, such as keeping cats strictly indoors. The prospective buyer of a condominium should determine beforehand whether keeping animals is prohibited and what the rules are if they are permitted.

22. Determining its age: How old is a cat in human terms?

A linear conversion, by saying that one cat year equals seven human years, is not really a valid way of looking at the cat's aging process. In the first months of life, a cat develops very rapidly, and then it remains almost at the same level of fitness and agility for many years. In the last stage of its life, however, it ages relatively quickly. In numbers, a five-month-old kitten corresponds to an 8-year-old human child, while a one-year-old cat is the equivalent of a 14-year-old

EQUIPMENT AND ACCESSORIES

By providing the right equipment, you ensure that the cat will be comfortable in your household. A cat-friendly home environment offers your pet plenty of opportunities for exercise

SLEEPING ARRANGEMENTS
You must provide warmth and security for your cats. Don't choose a bed that's too small, and make sure the coverings can be removed and washed (see overview, page 30).

CAT DOOR
Various models and sizes are available from specialty stores, for installation in doors and walls. An electromagnetic cat door is coded to open for your cat alone.

LITTER BOX
The litter box must be large enough to accommodate the cat comfortably. Various models range from simple plastic pans to more elaborate boxes with privacy hoods.

SCRATCH BOARD
Cats need an opportunity to sharpen their claws. A scratch board or scratching post is ideal for this purpose.

CAT LEASH
Collar (reflective, with address tag) or harness, retractable leash for a wider radius of action.

WINDOW PERCH
A windowsill seat or extension is ideal for a cat that wants to gaze at the world outdoors. It is especially important for indoor cats that never go out.

and play and also keeps it from getting into mischief. Sensible, appropriate accessories make daily routines, grooming, and health maintenance easier.

CAT GRASS
Cat grass is available as a grass-growing kit in specialty stores. The grass grows within only a few days. It is now also sold in tubes in gel form, containing all the important vitamins.

TOYS
Balls (including snack balls and catnip balls), toy mice, squeaky animals, feather toys, play tunnels, and rustling cushions will keep your pet occupied.

BRUSHES AND COMBS
You will need a small-tooth comb (with ultra-close tooth spacing), a wide-tooth comb for long hair, and a brush with natural bristles.

PET CARRIER
A pet carrier made of plastic with a metal door, ideally a top-loading model, is sturdy, shock-resistant, and easy to clean.

CAT MEDICINE CHEST
A pet medicine chest is useful for treating minor injuries, taking care of sick animals, and providing first aid in emergencies (see overview, page 136).

FOOD AND WATER BOWLS
Made of stainless steel or lead-free ceramics, bowls should be heavy and stable. Provide a separate bowl or dish for each cat. Good idea: A rubber ring will make the bowl skid-proof.

THE BEST FAMILY CATS

**Family life is not always tranquil. There is no place for highly
sensitive cats that quickly get panicky and hide under the
armoire whenever things get hectic or the children are making**

ABYSSINIAN
Curious, playful cat that loves to climb and
poses no problem even for first-time cat
owners.

BIRMAN
Gentle, even-tempered, and highly companionable cat. Attractive breed with an elegant
coat and white "gloves.

BRITISH SHORTHAIR
Keeps its cool and remains friendly even in the
midst of chaos. This breed is not inclined to
leap around wildly, so it also makes a good
indoor pet.

EUROPEAN SHORTHAIR
Looks like a normal housecat and is just as
robust, affectionate, and easy to care for.
Loves to stalk.

CHARTREUX
Impressive breed with an unmistakable vel-
vety coat of bluish fur. Quiet, reserved, and
low-maintenance.

MAINE COON
Large, powerfully built beauty with a semi-
long coat. Eager to go outdoors even in foul
weather. Friendly and quiet.

noise. In demand are even-tempered and sociable animals that are not easily rattled. Here you will learn about the best pedigreed cats for families.

NORWEGIAN FOREST CAT
Rugged breed whose thick coat can stand up to any weather. Independent, but devoted and even-tempered.

RAGDOLL
Gentle and lovable, always patient, even with children. The bright blue eyes are a striking feature.

RUSSIAN BLUE
Slender cat with a thick, soft coat whose struc-ture differs from that of other shorthaired breeds. Low-maintenance, gentle.

SOMALI
Semi-longhaired relative of the Abyssinian. Like its cousin, active, interested in every-thing, and always ready to play.

TONKINESE
Even-tempered, friendly shorthaired breed; it is an excellent indoor cat and gets along well with other house pets.

TURKISH ANGORA
Elegant feline aristocrat with an attractive coat that needs regular grooming. Very devoted to its human, playful, and lively.

teen. At the age of 4, a cat corresponds to a 32-year-old human, and an 8-year-old cat, to a 48-year-old. At the age of 12, the cat is as old as we are at 64, and a 15-year-old cat is comparable to a 76-year-old human.

23. **Farm cat: The cat on a nearby farm has had kittens. Should I get a little kitty there?**

This is a question that can't be answered conclusively. On the one hand, you are offering a sheltered, comfortable home to a kitten that faces an uncertain future. On the other hand, you generally know little or nothing about the new protégé of your choice—especially if no one on the farm looks after the cats and they are semiferal. Kittens that have been handled by humans will adjust better to life as a pet. Often the animals have inadequate veterinary care or none at all, and they are not protected against infections. If the mother cat has to fend for herself and forage for food, she only rarely will enter into a closer relationship with humans, and this behavior will be passed on to her young. If you decide on a farm kitten, its heart and kidneys must be examined by a veterinarian, and it must have the necessary inoculations. The adjustment to your home, in any event, will be more difficult for the farm kitten than for a kitten that has been kept indoors and socialized to humans at a young age. As a general rule, you will need previous experience in dealing with cats.

Farm cats often have little contact with humans and require plenty of empathy and patience.

24. **Inheritance:** **Can I include my cats in my will as beneficiaries?**

Animals are treated as property under the law and, therefore, may not be included in your will as direct heirs.

To provide for your cats in advance, you can require your heirs to care for the animals by means of a testamentary disposition. Alternatively, you can set up a foundation and make funds or nonmonetary resources available, for example, for a society for the prevention of cruelty to cats, which then will also look after your cats.

25. **Legal liability:** **Do I need to take out a special legal liability policy for my cat?**

An animal owner is responsible for any damage done by his pet to persons or property. This is all the more reason to keep your cat indoors and under supervision at all times. There is no requirement for a special insurance policy for your cat, however.

26. **Life expectancy:** **What determines a cat's life expectancy?**

A healthy diet, meticulous grooming, and regular veterinary care ensure that domestic cats now live distinctly longer than they did just a few decades ago. Life expectancy is decisively affected by lifestyle: Indoor cats can live to be 12 to 15 years old, sometimes even 20 or more, while statistics show that indoor-outdoor cats live only half that long. Studies in Sweden and France came to alarming conclusions: The average life expectancy of free-roaming male cats was only 3 years, that of females no more than 4. Castration or spaying has a positive effect on life expectancy, since neutered animals are much more domesticated and have little inclination to roam.

27. Litter box: What features are important in choosing a litter box for my cat?

The litter box needs to be large enough so that the cat has room to turn around easily. A high rim will keep litter from being kicked out into the room. For young cats, a container with lower sides is easier to climb in and out of. Models with a hood and a swinging door are usually equipped with a filter system. Nevertheless, ventilation problems can arise, and they may keep sensitive cats from using the box. In buying litter, you can choose among clumping varieties, filler, made of absorbent clay, a silica gel granulate that absorbs large quantities of liquid, and a plant-based, biodegradable cat litter. Let the cat decide which litter is most appealing. Soiled litter must be removed daily, and the box should be thoroughly cleaned once a week.

28. Microchip: What are the reasons for identifying your cat with a microchip?

Implantation of a microchip gives the cat an internationally valid identification number (twelve-digit ID number and three-digit country code), which can be used to reliably identify it. The veterinarian injects the minuscule (0.5×0.5 inch (12×12 mm)) transponder under the skin on the back of the neck; no anesthesia is necessary. The ID number is read with a special scanner that veterinarians, animal shelters, and often breed clubs also have. For registered cats, microchip implantation improves the chance of finding a lost animal.

29. Names: What names can cats hear best?

Open vowels are most easily heard by cats. One- and two-syllable names with "a" or "i" are well suited for everyday use. And the name need not always be Fluffy or Mitzi if you want a spur for your imagination, the manual *1000 Cat Names* (see Books, page 239) will provide you with a host of unusual suggestions. The name should sound loving and gentle, so that the cat links it with something pleasant. If the kitty misbehaves, don't use its name to scold it, in order to avoid endangering the positive association. Cats have minds of their own. If they're not in the mood, even the prettiest name won't get them to budge.

30. **Neighborhood law: Do I have to keep our cat off our neighbor's property if he insists on it?**

Every locality enacts its own laws to deal with issues of animals roaming loose. If you own a cat, you should familiarize yourself with these laws and abide by them accordingly. While some localities, especially rural areas, have no restrictions on allowing cats to roam, more populated areas are requiring cat licenses or levying fines and other measures to restrict free-roaming animals.

If your cat damages another person's property, you can be held responsible if the person decides to make a case of it, particularly if you are in violation of local ordinance by letting your cat roam. That seems reason enough not to let your cat go outdoors unsupervised.

1 *One- and two-syllable names with "a" and "i" are easiest for cats to hear. Call your cat in a gentle voice.*

2 *During training, if the cat comes when called, a treat will reinforce the name's positive meaning.*

PLACES TO SLEEP AND REST

For cats, their bed is more than a place to snooze and dream about mice. It is the center of their home territory and their personal property, to which no one has access; it offers

THERMAL CUSHION

This body cushion is filled with polyester fibers that store heat for a long time and insulate against cold floors. The cushion is washable and easy to transport. Standard size: 16 × 24 inches (40 × 60 cm). It is also good as a "secondary residence."

SNUGGLE SACK

This 2-feet (60-cm)-long snuggly bed in the shape of a sack (diameter of opening: about 12 inches (30 cm)) has an especially cozy, soft inner lining. When the cat doesn't want to be disturbed, it can burrow inside this den and hide.

NEST BED

The feline home is ideal for lazing about and dreaming. It comes with extra-high side walls, a soil-resistant textile cover, a zipper system, and a side pocket. The winter bed has a plush cover, and the summer bed is covered with fabric.

refuge, warmth, and a feeling of security. It's best to let the cat decide what it prefers: a cuddly cave, a cat basket, or a thermal cushion.

PARADISE OF WARMTH

This bed, which ensures comfort and warmth, can easily be suspended from all panel and finned radiators. The elevated vantage point gives the cat a sense of security. Bed surface: 18 × 13 inches (46 × 34 cm). The cover is removable and washable and comes in a variety of colors.

COZY CAVE

Cats love caves and hideaways. A sleeping cave with a plush lining and soft cushion is exactly to a cat's taste. Choose a model that is easy to clean (vacuum), with a cushion and padding that are removable and machine-washable.

WICKER BASKET

The renowned wicker basket has been joined by more up-to-date versions such as an extravagant cat high-rise condo made of natural willow or a smart wicker house. Keeping the wickerwork clean is more complicated than maintaining smooth materials.

31. Purebred cats: Why is a purebred cat frequently so expensive?

Depending on the breed, ancestry, and appearance, purebred cats cost roughly $500 to $1,000. What many a would-be buyer sees as exorbitant, proves on closer inspection to be not excessive at all. The breeder incurs high expenses until the kittens are ready to go to new homes at the age of 12 or 13 weeks:

➤ Stud fee for male: $20, sometimes even more
➤ Blood test for mother cat: $100
➤ Kitten food and cat litter: $160 per animal
➤ Veterinary expenses for initial examination with certificate, basic series of immunizations, worm treatments: about $210
➤ Papers (pedigree) from the breed association: $25
➤ Additional expenses for any delivery problems and illnesses; increased food requirements of the mother cat during pregnancy and nursing phase; trips, attendance at shows, accessories (toys), telephone calls, and placement of ads

The breeder's actual costs for a carefully reared, healthy young animal generally exceed $500. Don't go near purebred kittens that cost substantially less. They may come from questionable breeding operations, often are not vaccinated, may have inadequate veterinary care, and as a result may develop behavioral disturbances.

32. Purebred cats: How does a purebred cat differ from non-purebred members of its species?

Unlike non-purebred cats, purebreds possess certain characteristics that are the result of selective breeding. These include physical features such as physique, head shape, hair length, hair structure, coat color, and coat marking, as well as character-related and behavioral attributes. The characteristics are common to all animals of the breed and are passed on to their offspring. Within most breeds there are subcategories (varieties), for which particular characteristics are mandatory (for example, various color standards). The breed characteristics are set forth in the breed standard.

33. Registration: **What advantages will I gain from having my cat registered?**

If you want to show your cat in a recognized show, then you must register it with the association sponsoring the show. This typically requires some paperwork and a fee. The pedigree you receive is proof of your pet's lineage. Some shows have categories for non-purebred household pets, but these, too, must be registered with the appropriate association before they can be shown. Breeders must also register their breeding stock in order to register the kittens that they produce.

34. Right of return: **What options do I have if there are serious problems with my new cat?**

In the sales contract, a right of return should be agreed on, in case unforeseeable problems make it unduly difficult or impossible to house the cat adequately. This may be the case, for example, if other pets vehemently protest the addition to the family and perhaps even endanger the cat's health. Generally the right of return is limited to a specific time period. A seller who is concerned with the cat's well-being will regardless of the contractual provision join the buyer in looking for a mutually acceptable solution if emergencies arise at a

INFO

Cat allergy
Cats can cause allergic reactions in humans, ranging from tearing eyes and a runny nose to respiratory distress. The allergy is caused by dander (flakes of dried skin and saliva), which the cat spreads when it cleans its coat. The allergens linger in the air for a long time. Regularly wiping the coat with a damp chamois can help alleviate the symptoms. If intense reactions occur, however, often the only solution is to part with the cat.

later date. A good breeder (see page 16) will not break off contact with the owners of his animals in any event and will always be ready to discuss minor and major issues concerning the keeping of the cat.

35. Safety netting: What should a practical safety net for a cat look like?

A balcony safety net for the cat must be tear-proof, made of environmentally friendly material, resistant to UV radiation, and rot-proof. Unsuitable are nets with a mesh size larger than 1.3 inches (35 mm) because the cat could get its head caught in the mesh. Ideal are firmly knotted nets, which don't allow shifting. Cat safety nets are sold in various widths and lengths and can easily be cut to the desired size and securely attached with a tensioning rope. Thanks to their muted colors, the nets are almost invisible. If you live in a rented apartment, you should get the landlord's permission before putting up the netting; condo owners need the agreement of the owners' association.

36. The sale: What is the legal basis for buying and selling a cat?

Basically, as in horse trading, it's "buyer beware." Do your homework beforehand. Avoid inexperienced "backyard breeders" and stores that may be getting their animals from dubious operations called "kitten mills." These types of breeders are interested only in turning quick profits, not in placing healthy animals in loving homes. On the other hand, reputable breeders are interested in promoting and improving the quality of their chosen breed, and they care about their kittens' future. They will often screen prospective buyers to make sure the person can offer a suitable home environment for their kitten. This type of breeder is typically aligned with a particular cat association and participates in cat shows, which are, by the way, good places to look for experienced, professional breeders.

Certainly, the buyer has a right to expect a healthy animal, but must also understand that no absolute guarantees can be placed on a living creature. The sale should be accompanied by a contract that spells out any warranty period or terms under which the buyer can return the cat and request all or a portion of his money back. The contract should also state what the buyer is entitled to if defects are found later in the animal (such as dental flaws, joint diseases, worm infestation). Should a dispute arise later, having a written agreement signed by both parties is vital to defending your position in the matter.

37. Sales contract: What should be set forth in the contract when buying a cat?

A sales contract determines the rights and duties of buyer and seller. It should contain this information:
➤ Names and addresses of buyer and seller
➤ Sex, age, color, and any special distinguishing features of the cat
➤ Condition when sold (state of health, vaccinations, worm treatments)
➤ Trial period or right of return, in case unforeseen problems appear
➤ Warranty terms
➤ Notation of the surrender of vaccination certificate to the buyer
➤ Purchase price, perhaps with method of payment
➤ Provision for failure to meet obligation (handover, payment)
➤ Place, date, signatures of buyer and seller

EXTRA TIP

Lost Cat!
Emergency plan, if your cat has disappeared:
➤ Search the entire house from attic to cellar.
➤ Inform animal shelters within a 30-mile (50-km) radius.
➤ Ask neighbors, animal control officers, the regulatory agency, the fire department, the road maintenance staff.
➤ Post flyers (with photo) in stores, supermarkets (bulletin board), and veterinarians' offices.
➤ Put a classified ad in the local newspaper.

Additional contractual issues for purebred cats:
➤ Name and cattery name, breed, color, parents, number in breed registry
➤ Pet-quality cat, show cat, or breeding cat
➤ Guarantee of lineage
➤ Rights of preemption and redemption

38. **Seriors and cats: Can keeping a cat be recommended without reservations for elderly people?**

A cat is an ideal partner for older people. Especially for seniors who live alone, it is the right "medicine": A cat requires devotion and responsibility, brings life into the house, bolsters sinking spirits, and keeps people mobile. The relationship with their protégé often causes many seniors to become more open to their surroundings again and make new contacts with other people, because an animal always provides a topic for conversation. A cat for senior citizens must be especially companionable and gentle (see Cats for Singles and Seniors, page 37). Generally an adult cat is preferable because taking care of a kitten takes a great deal of time and physical effort. To guarantee that the cat will be looked after during the owner's illness or after his/her death, sponsorship or adoption should be arranged in advance. Retirement homes and nursing homes increasingly are willing to allow animals to be kept or brought for visits.

39. **Sexing: What is the difference between male and female cats?**

The female's vaginal opening is a vertical slit located directly below the anus. The male's testicles are found between the anus and the round opening where the tip of the penis is concealed. Gentle pressure beneath the opening will cause the penis to emerge. In a young male, the testicles are visible only as a slight bulge.

CATS FOR SINGLES AND SENIORS

For many singles and seniors, a cat is an important part of life. Some people want a high-spirited relationship, while others are looking for a sweet temper and affection.

BURMESE
Demanding and vivacious breed. Requires devotion and activity. For singles with plenty of time and love to offer.

EXOTIC SHORTHAIR
Cross between American Shorthair and Persian. Devoted and deliberate in temperament. Ideal partner for senior citizens.

JAVANESE
Wide-awake and sensitive, requires constant company. Attractive silky coat with moderate need for grooming. For singles and seniors.

PERSIAN
Lovable and quiet, with a well-balanced temperament. Luxuriant long hair with thick undercoat that needs daily grooming.

REX
Playful and devoted purebred cat with curly or wavy coat. Because of its short coat, it usually is best kept as an indoor cat.

SIAMESE
Very demanding and communicative breed, but often headstrong as well. For singles with experience and the right touch with cats.

40. Tattooing: Is it still advisable these days to have a cat tattooed?

Until the introduction of the microchip, tattooing was the standard permanent identification method. But a tattoo has real disadvantages. To spare the animal pain, it has to be anesthetized during the tattooing, but with the microchip that is unnecessary. The tattooed number is not forgery-proof, it fades and often becomes illegible, and the return of runaway animals is problematic. Thus everything speaks in favor of a decision to use microchip identification for your cat.

Species-Appropriate Care

For a cat, home has special significance. In this chapter, you'll learn what makes an environment appropriate for a cat and where your cat makes special demands on living arrangements in the home you share.

41. Bed: **My cat sleeps in my bed. Should I forbid it to do this for reasons of hygiene?**

Cats are among the cleanest animals in the world. A healthy cat is painstaking in its grooming habits. From the hygienic standpoint, there is nothing wrong with sleeping in your bed provided you don't object to cat hair on the sheets. If you're a light sleeper, keep in mind that a cat gets up repeatedly between the different phases of sleep. When the children go to bed, the cat has to leave the room; it should not be allowed in a child's bed. And don't forget, please: If you let your cat sleep in your bed and change your mind later, you're asking for unnecessary trouble.

42. Boarding: **How can I tell whether my cat is happy where it's being boarded?**

If the following requirements are met, you can leave your cat with a pet boarding service with a clear conscience:

➤ All the animals being boarded look healthy and clean.

➤ Only vaccinated and wormed animals are accepted as boarders.

➤ The cages and outdoor runs are cleaned daily.

➤ The cats are kept in separate cages, but have visual contact with each other.

➤ Each cat has its own outdoor run, protected from rain.

➤ All the animals can look outdoors.

➤ The sleeping room is securely locked at night.

➤ A heated area (infrared light, underfloor heating) protects the animals against cold.

➤ There are scratching posts for sharpening claws.

➤ The food bowls are clean.

➤ The cats are fed commercially available cat food.

➤ The caretakers are intensely involved in the cats' care and also take time to play with them.

➤ Health checks are performed by a veterinarian who pays regular visits.

➤ The cat is allowed to have its favorite toys, which make the boarding experience more pleasant.
➤ The operator of the boarding service has proof of expertise or excellent recommendations.

43. Bottom-hung windows: **Why are bottom-hung windows so dangerous for cats?**

A cat proves itself to be extremely shrewd when it comes to finding a way to get outdoors. If nobody will let it out the door and there's no cat door that permits an unhindered escape, a window that's tilted open is just the thing. The plan to squeeze through the narrow opening, however, often ends with the kitty getting stuck in the gap, which narrows toward the bottom, and being unable to get free. Vigorous attempts at extrication only cause it to slip farther down. Even if the wedged-in cat is freed in good time, nerves in its hindquarters frequently are seriously crushed, and paralysis can result. Prevent these potentially fatal campaigns by installing special safety gratings for bottom-hung windows, available in specialty stores.

44. Breeding: **I want to breed my Siamese. How do I get started?**

As a breeder, you should have a basic knowledge of your animals' anatomy and behavior, the breeding requirements, breed standards, and the most important laws of genetics. Breeding requires plenty of room: you can't keep a breeding group in a two-room apartment, and a breeding stud has to be separated from the other animals from time to time. Ideal conditions for breeding cats are provided by a house with a screened enclosure from which the animals can't escape. Breeding takes time: Taking care of several cats and their young can't be combined with a normal full-time job. Some compromises will be called for when it comes to leisure activities and vacation and travel plans. Breeding takes money: A responsible cat breeder can't make any money by breeding cats. Besides the basic veterinary care and required shots, a single infection in your breeding stock often is extremely costly. In addition, there are the costs of equipment, accessories/supplies, trips to shows and courses for breeders, and much more.

45. Care: **Can I occasionally leave my cat home alone over the weekend?**

Cats are loners, but regular social contact is indispensable for them. Moreover, a cat bonds more closely with its owner than with other cats. This also means that you shouldn't leave the kitty alone for more than a few hours. If you're out all day, want to go off for a weekend, or plan to go away on vacation, you need to arrange in advance for someone to take care of the cat and give it regular attention. Indoor-outdoor cats handle time alone better than indoor cats, and boredom also is less likely with two cats in the house. Start practicing leaving your pet alone occasionally while it is still a kitten.

46. Care: **What should a cat-appropriate home provide?**

Here are some recommendations for the housing of domestic cats indoors:
➤ Readily available floor space: at least 738 square feet (225 m^2) for one or two cats.

➤ Ceiling height: at least 6.5 feet (2 m)

➤ Room temperature: 61 to 75°F (16 to 24°C)

➤ Lighting conditions: 350 to 450 Lux

➤ Atmospheric humidity: 50 to 60%

➤ The rooms must be draft-free.

➤ The room structure and furnishings, including bookshelves and wall shelving, should allow the cat to sit or lie at various heights and to have access to hideaways.

➤ The cat should be able to choose

The cat makes a daily inspection of its living area and territory. It should learn from the outset to respect taboo zones.

between at least two places to rest and sleep.

➤ Each cat has a food bowl and a water bowl.

➤ Each cat has a litter box; even better is an additional box elsewhere in the home.

➤ The feeding area and the litter box are not directly next to each other.

➤ The cat can sharpen its claws on an easily accessible scratching post or scratch boards.

➤ Cat-appropriate toys satisfy its hunting instinct and need for exercise.

➤ If kept indoors exclusively, the cat needs an opportunity to observe its environment through a window.

➤ All bottom-hung windows are secured with a special safety device.

➤ Balconies and windows above the first floor are made secure with safety screens.

➤ Potential sources of danger are removed or made inaccessible to the cat.

➤ The cat has at least 6 hours of daily contact with its human.

47. Care: Our cat is allowed to go into every room. Now I read that this is wrong. Why?

A loner like the cat defines its territory and expects the same of others. Cats need boundaries; unlimited freedom is not in the cat's nature. Taboo zones and prohibited areas in your home should be defined as soon as the cat moves in. If your pet is consistently kept out of the bedroom or utility room (because of the cleaning agents and chemicals), it rarely will get into mischief. But it is also part of a cat's self-image to protest against taboos from time to time and to deliberately provoke a border violation. If you are firm, the event will quickly be over. But if you rescind the cat's agreed-upon rights and issue subsequent prohibitions (for example, by declaring the bed off limits), you will not win your pet's friendship.

48. Cat door: Should I install a little cat door to let my cat go out?

Before wondering about giving the cat its own door, you need to decide whether you should be letting it go outdoors at all. Apart from that, a cat door offers definite advantages: The cat can go in and out at will and doesn't get on your nerves by constantly meowing at the front door. If necessary (for example, if you don't want kitty out at night), the door can simply be locked. Door models with an electronic lock react only to the transmitter worn on the cat's safety col-

INFO

Poisonous plants
These house plants are poisonous for cats: alpine rose, cyclamen, azalea, bean, Christmas rose, dieffenbachia, ivy, wolfsbane, golden chain tree, hydrangea, calla lily, potato vine, arbor vitae, bay, lupine, lily of the valley, mistletoe, daffodil, oleander, spindle tree, philodendron, sweet pea, primrose, delphinium, tobacco, tomato, tulip, juniper, poinsettia, male fern.

lar, and strange cats stay outside. The cat will quickly grasp what the door is about, once you demonstrate how it works. If it takes a while to get the idea, call your pet from the other side of the door and provide a treat as a reward when the kitty has learned how to negotiate the passage.

Cat doors are available in various sizes and styles, for installation in doors or walls. Before you install one in a rented apartment, however, you need to confer with the landlord.

49. Cat sitter: **What is important when my cat is being taken care of by a sitter?**

The cat sitter will pay you a visit before you leave, to get acquainted with your pet and your home. For the sitter, this information is vital:

➤ Where is the cat food kept? Put a can opener out in plain sight.

➤ What are the cat's normal feeding times?

➤ Is there enough cat litter to last while you're gone?

➤ Where do you dispose of the soiled litter?

➤ Does the cat need to be combed and brushed?

➤ What is its favorite toy?

➤ Where is the pet carrier kept?

➤ Is the cat medicine chest (see overview, page 136) fully equipped and well stocked?

➤ Is the cat allowed to go outdoors? When should it stay in? Is there a cat door?

➤ Does the cat need regular medication or special food (for certain dietary needs)?

➤ Does it have special habits and peculiarities that the cat sitter has to bear in mind?

➤ Do other people have access to your home?

Leave the sitter your vacation address, including a telephone number, the address and phone number of your vet, the veterinary emergency clinic, and the pet shelter, as well as the name and address of a person to contact. The vaccination certificate should be kept handy. Give the sitter the door key, and leave an extra key with your neighbor or the contact person.

50. Children and cats: **Is it all right for small children to play unsupervised with cats?**

Children often are not entirely gentle with cats; they will pull their tails, clutch at their faces, hold their legs tightly, or try to push them flat on the floor. Even young children will learn the ground rules of getting along if you patiently explain to them the cat's behavior and needs. Nevertheless, don't leave them unsupervised with the kitty. Since children and cats usually play together at eye level, the risk of injury is high if the cat should ever defend itself with tooth and claw. And after such an experience, it can take a long time to overcome the fear of the supposedly "bad" animal. Not until the age of 11 or 12 are children capable of independently looking after the cat and caring for it properly.

51. Cleanliness: **In a household with a cat, where should special attention be given to cleanliness?**

In particular, the cat's bed and other sleeping places must be cleaned regularly to prevent fleas. Even if you only rarely see a flea on your cat's coat, this is not

1 Intent on the action, cats may employ their claws and teeth as well. When playing, therefore, children should not get too close.

2 Bosom buddies: Often a very special relationship of trust develops between children and cats.

absolute proof that your home is flea-free. Fleas go through various developmental stages, and the flea population consists of about 34% eggs, 57% larvae, 8% pupae, and no more than 1% adult fleas. Only mature fleas seek out a host to suck blood, while the great majority of the population stays in the cracks and cushions in the cat's bed. Cleaning the cat's living areas with a vacuum cleaner and flea spray (also spray inside the vacuum cleaner bag regularly) is at least as important as controlling the parasites on your pet itself. Even a mild flea infestation should always be taken seriously.

52.   Collar: **Will a collar with a little bell deter the cat from trying to hunt birds?**

The tiny bell on a cat's collar is useless: As a hunter that lies in wait, the cat advances furtively and slowly before overpowering its prey from up close. A little bell would not make a sound during this process. It is audible only when the cat is running freely through the terrain. And no alarm signal is needed then because all the birds in the surrounding area will have long since registered the cat's presence and loudly alerted each other to the danger. Collars with or without a bell are not totally risk-free for cats: While stalking through bushes, the cat can get caught and may be unable to free itself unaided. If a front paw slips through the collar while the cat is grooming its coat, an injury in the axillary area often results. For these reasons, when buying a flea collar or a decorative collar, choose only a break-away type that will open if enough pressure is applied.

53.   Daily routine: **Things are often hectic and noisy in our family. Will that make the cat suffer?**

Cats can be shrinking violets, but in many situations they prove to be more adaptable than we think. Even with loud music or noisy children nearby, a cat can relax completely and take a nap, and if things get too boisterous, it simply looks for a quieter place. However, it will show little understanding if everything in its environment is in disorder:

➤ if feeding schedules and joint play and cuddling times are not observed,

➤ if everybody in the family keeps coming home at constantly changing times,

➤ if it is constantly disturbed while sleeping,

➤ if its old rights are suddenly rescinded (such as sleeping in your bed or going outdoors),

➤ if it's become nothing more than a fifth wheel because other things are more important,

➤ if the furniture is rearranged,

➤ if the cat bed, litter box, and food dish keep being moved from one place to another.

54. Danger of falling: **How do I protect my cat against falling out of the window or off the balcony?**

Cats move with instinctive sureness and balance, without hesitation, even on a narrow balcony railing.

1 *It doesn't have to be a cat basket all the time: under the covers, too, your pet can be undisturbed when things get too chaotic in the household.*

2 *An awkward situation: If the cat feels uncomfortable in its setting, there are frequently problems with hygiene.*

But even cats are not immune from falling, and often a mere bird flying by is enough to make them throw all caution to the winds. Therefore your cat should be given access to the balcony only if it is secured with protective screening or netting. Cat safety nets are almost invisible, weather-resistant, tear-resistant; they can be cut to any length desired and are also suitable for securing verandas and patios. For doors and windows, there are special pet screens, resembling insect screens but with mesh that is much stronger and more stress-resistant. The screen, mounted in its own frame, is easy to install, and there is no need to drill holes in the window frame or wall.

55. Foster mother: **Where do I find a feline foster mother for orphaned kittens?**

A suitable substitute mother, or foster queen, for orphaned kittens is another mother cat that has given birth at the same time. The foster mom, however, should not nurse more kittens than she can manage along with her own. Generally the adoption is no problem, if the scent of the orphans' new mother (her urine, for example) is rubbed on them in advance. The best places to search for a foster mom are cat breeders' associations and possibly veterinarians' offices and pet shelters. The pronounced "fostering behavior" of the domestic cat has quite often saved the lives of other orphaned animals too. Cats have accepted even squirrels, hares, rabbits, foxes, and puppies of smaller breeds and served as their foster parents.

56. Going outdoors: **Is going outside on a regular basis an essential part of cat-appropriate care?**

Ever since cats and humans have lived under the same roof, there have been two opposing points of view: Some cat owners assume that only cats that can go outdoors are able to engage in the behaviors typical of their species, while other owners are convinced that

Don't let your cat go outdoors unless you live far from streets with heavy traffic. The danger of an accident would be too great.

indoor cats also are happy cats. The fact is that a cat living in a cat-appropriate home lacks for nothing. An exclusively indoor life, however, places an obligation on the cat owner: As the cat's attachment figure, he or she plays a special role. To a greater extent than a cat that goes outdoors, an indoor cat coordinates its daily routine to its owner's rhythm of life and expects him or her to adhere to fixed times for feeding, cuddling, and play. Going outdoors entails numerous risks, and an indoor cat's life expectancy is markedly greater. A cat that has been allowed outdoors will stage a massive protest if it suddenly is asked to live indoors exclusively, but adjustment is possible.

57. Going outdoors: **How can the risks for free-roaming cats be reduced, and what are the alternatives to letting them go outside?**

If congested streets are at all nearby, cats should never be allowed outdoors. Even side streets with little traffic can be dangerous, however, because the cat is not expecting cars and often will sit in the middle of the street. At night, let your cat out only if your property is bordered by gardens and fields. With a lockable cat door, you can control the times for going outside. Serve your cat its main meals at fixed times and always after its territorial patrol; that way it will quickly learn to come home on time. Protective screening, like that used for balcony safety is also suitable for yards and patios. Fresh air also can be had when you walk the cat on its leash, though not every cat takes well to leash-training. Females in heat and lovesick toms must be kept indoors. In the first weeks after a move, too, the cat should stay indoors.

58. Hierarchy: **Our two ruffians are six months old and always quarreling. Do I need to mediate?**

Wild wrangling between littermates is the order of the day at the awkward age. Even at this early stage, they're testing to see what is allowed and what is not, who is "top dog" and who has to give in. In the process, the boundaries between a game and a serious situation sometimes are blurred, and in the heat of combat the sharp little teeth do more than nip playfully. The one being tormented emits a loud squeal, and the opponent lets go. Even if the fur is flying, things are not so serious, and a few minutes later the fierce combatants are sleeping in their cat basket, snuggled close together. A human referee would just be in the way here.

HOUSEHOLD DANGERS

Source of Danger	How to Protect Your Cat
Aquarium	Cover to keep cat from falling in. Kittens are especially at risk.
Balcony	Secure with cat safety netting.
Bathtub	Never leave cat alone in bathroom when tub is full.
Bottom-hung windows	Secure with special pet safety screens (available in specialty stores).
Chemicals, varnish, and paint	Keep cleaning agents, solvents, thinners, and paints under lock and key.
Cooking area, toaster, stovetop	Allow cat in kitchen only when supervised, and never while cooking is going on.
Curtains	Kittens are at risk of falling; keep curtains raised in the first few weeks.
Doors	Door stoppers will prevent the cat from being caught in the door.
Electrical cables	Cover cables in which current flows.
Garbage cans	Cover garbage containers with lids.
House plants	Remove plants poisonous to cats.
Medications	Harmful, even toxic (aspirin and acetaminophen). Keep locked away.
Open fire	Attach safety screen to front of fireplace. Put out candles if the cat will be alone.
Plastic bags	Never leave lying around open. The cat can get tangled up in them and suffocate.
Sharp objects	Put needles, scissors, thumbtacks away.
Small objects	Buttons, paperclips, etc., are easy to swallow. Keep them out of reach.
Stairs	Block stairs, platforms, and exits with child safety gates.
Sump pumps	Keep covered. Small kittens can fall in and drown.
Swimming pools	Cats can swim but can't climb out and will drown from exhaustion.
Washing machine	Close loading hatch after use.

59. Kitty litter: I've bought a new kind of litter, but it doesn't meet with my tom's approval. What's his problem?

Cats react very individually to the litter in their box. Basically unsuitable is any filler with pointed and sharp-edged particles, in which a cat is reluctant to scratch. Generally cats also will not accept dusty and scented varieties. In addition to the clumping litters made of absorbent clay material, there is silica gel litter, whose granulate also soaks up large quantities of liquid and absorbs odors especially well. Specialty stores also sell fully biodegradable cat litter made of recycled products. Test them to see which cat litter your pet prefers.

60. Litter box: What can cause the cat to stop using its litter box?

Cats are creatures of habit that retain certain preferences. If your cat is allowed outdoors every day and is in the habit of relieving itself while outside, it will use the box only when it has to stay indoors for an extended period. Usually there is an attractive bathroom site outdoors, with soft earth or sand, that the cat regularly heads for.

INFO

What are the costs of keeping a cat?
In addition to the recurring costs for cat food, litter, and routine vaccinations, there are additional expenses for the veterinarian, cat sitter or boarding service (sums in euros, for one cat): food, $40–$50 per month; cat litter, $25–$35 per month; veterinarian, about $50–$65 annually for check-ups and shots; cat sitter, $5–$25 per visit; cat boarding service, $8–$10 per day. Other expenses: equipment and accessories.

If the cat resolutely avoids its litter box, there may be very different reasons for this:

➤ Unclean litter box: Cats react sensitively to odors and mess. Used litter must be removed daily, and the box should be cleaned thoroughly once a week.

➤ Box with hood: A litter box with a hood and door offers the cat the desired privacy, but unpleasant odors quickly form underneath the hood. When buying a litter box, choose a style with adequate ventilation and a filter system.

➤ Wrong location: Cats want to use the toilet unobserved and undisturbed, if at all possible. The right location is a quiet, draft-free corner of a room. Also make sure that the food bowl is not nearby.

➤ Litter: Not every type of cat litter will be accepted.

➤ Disease: As a result of diseases of the kidney and bladder, urination frequently is painful. Since the pain appears when the cat uses the litter box, the animal often associates the discomfort with the box and stays away from it.

➤ Behavior: Soiling indoors can be a sign of protest, when the cat's world is out of kilter. Typical triggers: neglect, "jealousy," loss or change of caregiver, move, oppression by other cats.

61. Moving: **We're about to move. How do I make sure that my cat handles the move well?**

Moving is a dramatic event for a cat because it signifies the loss of the animal's home territory. Here's how to manage the stress: Empty a room and reserve it for the cat. Keep it here with its basket, litter box, and food and water bowls until the packers have left. The cat should be the last to move into the new home; here too, leave your pet in one room until the hullabaloo in the rest of the house has died down. Later, let the cat begin its inspection tour. In the first 3 to 4 weeks, don't let your pet go outdoors at all.

62. Need to move around: **Is there a minimum size for apartments with a cat?**

The apartment should be no smaller than 738 square feet (225 m²). Much more important than the size of the area, however, is the structure of the living space: cats live in the third dimension. Sleeping places, vantage points, and hideaways at various levels (for example, in bookshelves or on wall shelving) that are reachable via jumping platforms, little ladders, or climbing trees increase the available space to move around in and offer retreats and hiding places, which are especially important if you keep two or more cats, for times when they want to stay out of each other's way.

63. Neutering: **At what age can a cat be castrated or spayed?**

The best time to spay a female is shortly before or after her first heat, that is, depending on the breed, between the sixth and eighth months of life. Males, too, should be castrated at the onset of sexual maturity (up to about 9 months). In the surgery, the vet anesthetizes the animal and removes the female's ovaries or the male's testicles (see Info, page 148). Neutering at this age has no harmful effect on either physical development or behavior; only in isolated instances does slight incontinence result. The operation distinctly reduces the incidence of breast tumors, by

EXTRA TIP

Adjusting to the car
Once the cat accepts its pet carrier as a second home, you can start getting it used to the car: Put the carrier, with the cat in it, on the back seat, strap a seat belt around the carrier, and speak in a soft voice to calm it. Do this repeatedly, also with the motor running. Drive only short distances on the first trial runs, and don't speed up or brake abruptly. Having a second person in the car will make the cat feel more secure.

almost 90% in comparison with non-neutered animals. Cats that are neutered substantially earlier sometimes remain smaller and are less likely to put on fat. In feral cats, the animal protection associations quite often perform such early operations at the age of 7–12 weeks, to safeguard against uncontrolled reproduction of the strays. In the United States, early neutering has been practiced for quite awhile. It is a way to decisively reduce both the risk of injury, because the neutered animals are less aggressive and far less apt to get into fights, and the risk of mutual communication of infectious diseases. Studies on possible consequences of early neutering for senior cats remain to be done.

64. Old cats: **How do the needs of older cats differ from those of younger ones?** ?

The first signs of aging appear when a cat is approximately 8 years old. These are the typical symptoms:
➤ The cat shows signs of reduced agility; it is less apt to jump and climb and has less desire to play wildly and for prolonged periods.
➤ It sleeps more. Indoor-outdoor cats increasingly dispense with hunting in their territory.
➤ It has a greater need for warmth.
➤ Despite a healthy, age-appropriate diet, the coat of many senior cats loses some of its glossiness.
➤ Its sight and hearing are less keen.
➤ Age-related complaints include digestive and kidney problems, and sometimes also periodontal problems, loss of teeth, and bad breath.
➤ Even if their appetite remains normal, old cats often lose weight.
When the cat senses that its mobility and overall fitness are decreasing, its behaviors and needs change:
➤ It becomes more obstinate and categorically rejects any changes in its daily routine.
➤ It shows less tolerance toward other cats and sometimes avoids them in order to conceal its weaknesses.
➤ It becomes more finicky about its food and will not accept a change in its diet.
➤ It avoids loud, noisy people and keeps its distance from children.

➤ It is anything but gracious if disturbed while resting.

➤ The bond with the humans it trusts becomes closer, it is more home-loving and fond of cuddling and makes demands for more closeness and devotion.

65. Poisonous plants: **Do cats instinctively avoid all plants that might pose a danger to them?**

A young cat's urge to nibble does not stop even at plants that can poison it. Adult cats behave more cautiously, but poisonous plants can be a danger for them as well, if you fail to supply them with green plants suitable for nibbling, such as cat grass, thyme, or parsley. To play it safe, banish all poisonous house plants (see Info, page 46) from your home.

66. Purebred cats: **What conditions must be met if I want to participate in shows with my Oriental Shorthair?**

At cat shows, purebred cats (in so-called household pet classes, however, non-purebred animals can also take part) are exhibited and judged and awarded prizes in various classes. The host is a breed association, which also determines the conditions for participation. Your Oriental must be listed in the breed registry and must have a pedigree as proof of its lineage. It participates in the individual class that corresponds to its age, for which it has the required title. The registration form is available from the show organizer. A registration fee is due when you receive confirmation of registration. These are the other requirements: Your cat must be free of disease, fungal infection, and parasites and must have been vaccinated against rabies, feline parvovirus, and cat flu. The vaccination certificates or health certificate are checked before the show starts. During the event, the cats stay in their cages. Honorary prizes and ribbons are awarded (in other countries, there is prize money as well). Breed associations can tell you where shows are held, but the locations are also published in daily newspapers and in magazines for cat fanciers.

67. Rearing: **What has happened when a mother cat refuses to take care of her young?**

Mother cats are good mothers; they look after their young lovingly. Problems with rearing their offspring are rare. Possible causes include illness, turbulence, stress, or the mother's inexperience.

➤ First-time mothers sometimes fail to take care of their young because they are overwhelmed and don't know what to do with the kittens.

➤ If the birthing box is constantly being disturbed, the mother cat is subjected to stress. Usually she will try to carry her kittens to a quiet, protected spot. In isolated cases, however, she sometimes will leave her young or direct her aggressive behavior, which actually is designed to ward off enemies, against her own kittens.

➤ With large litters, there may not be enough milk for all the kittens, and after a Caesarean section there may be no milk at all. If the cat is suffering from inflamed teats, she should not nurse her young. In any case, help must be quickly provided. The best solution is a feline wet nurse as a foster mother. Otherwise the only solution is to hand-rear the kittens with queen's milk, which requires experience and a great deal of time and energy, with feedings every 2 hours.

68. Rearing: **Should the mother cat and her young be kept separate from other cats?**

In the first, strenuous days after delivery, the mother cat should be spared any excitement. This applies particularly to visitors at the birthing box. The cat will react with extraordinary aggression to all strange cats, especially to strange toms. Even other cats living under the same roof with her should approach the young only if she trusts them. There are cases, however, in which the mother cat will let her offspring be taken care of temporarily by a female feline friend or even a male cat that she is especially fond of. Irrespective of this, the mother should be left alone with her kittens if she so requires. For this purpose, a separate room for her and her litter is the best solution.

69. Scratching post: **My cat is allowed to go out at any time of day or night. Does it still need a scratching post indoors?**

The scratching post is more than a place to sharpen claws. It expands the space available for the cat to move around in your home, invites climbing (otherwise the furniture would get used for this), ensures that the cat can keep track of things from an elevated observation post, and provides places for rest and retreat. And although the kitty sharpens its claws outdoors, it still wants to do so indoors as well and the sofa, armchairs, and rugs will quickly be in bad shape if no scratching post is available. Besides, a scratching post is an ideal place for games and gymnastics, if you equip it with a climbing rope, a feather toy, or a bungee mouse on a cord (see The Best Cat Toys, page 224).

70. Scratching post: **What kind of scratching post do I need, so that the cat will accept it?**

The scratch tree must be stable and sturdy and have a resistant, coarse surface texture (such as sisal or carpet). If it has special scratching areas, they should be positioned high enough to allow the cat to extend its body fully, with its front legs outstretched, when sharpening its claws. A scratching post that reaches to the ceiling (tension rod) offers excellent opportunities for climbing. Cats adore elevated perches, so hideaways and resting places at several levels on the scratching post are popular. The location is the decisive factor: A scratching post that is secluded in a corner will only rarely be used.

71. Sex drive: What is the best way for my queen to get through the stressful heat phase?

Most queens first go into heat (estrus) between the fifth and seventh months of life, when their ovaries produce eggs that can be fertilized. If the cat is not mated, she will continue to be in heat for up to 3 weeks, and this may recur two to four times a year, more often if she is an indoor cat. At this time she is strikingly eager to cuddle, eats almost nothing, rolls around on the floor, calls, whines, wanders around restlessly, and tries to get outdoors to look for a tom (see Info, page 65). Some cats in heat can be distracted, at least temporarily, by offers of exercise and play, while stroking and cuddling only reinforce their wish to mate. Keep the windows and doors securely closed to keep her from running off. To spare the cat (and yourself) this stress, have her spayed as soon as possible. Altering (see Info, page 148) is the best choice for all cats that are not intended for use in breeding.

72. Sleeping: How much sleep do cats need?

As slugabeds, cats are suspected of holding the world record; they can easily spend 16 hours a day asleep. Various sleep phases follow one another in succession. Basically, we distinguish between REM sleep and non-REM sleep. Non-REM sleep is broken down into various phases with different depths of sleep. Typical of the REM phase are eye movements beneath closed lids (REM = rapid eye movement). After a light sleep

Cats are world record holders when it comes to sleeping, and they always can find a suitable little spot for a siesta wherever they are.

phase lasting up to half an hour, the cat briefly falls into a deep sleep. Now it is completely relaxed and barely reacts to outside stimuli, while in light sleep it wakes immediately upon hearing unusual noises (such as the scampering of a mouse). REM sleep is the dream phase. Some researchers assume that the pattern of the eye movements is related to the dream images. You usually can tell a cat is dreaming by the twitching of its whiskers, mouth, and paws.

73. **Sleeping: What are the characteristics of a cat's ideal spot to rest and sleep?**

Very important for the cat's sleeping place is the location: if at all possible, somewhat off the main traffic paths in the household, but still in a spot where the cat can keep an eye on everything going on around it.
➤ The surface must be large enough for the cat to really stretch out and loll.
➤ The mattress, pillows, and covers provide cozy warmth and protect against cold rising up from the floor.
➤ The covers of the cushions and pillows must be removable and easy to clean, as well as machine-washable at a temperature of 140 or 200°F (60 or 95°C).
➤ Smooth materials are easier to keep clean than a wicker basket, for example.
➤ Specialty stores sell a wide range of different styles—from simple mats to plush caves and exclusive sleeping sofas (see overview, pages 30/31). Quite a number of cats, however, have ideas of their own when it comes to choosing their primary residence: One may love the cardboard box it arrived in, now slightly the worse for wear, while another is fond of a simple fruit crate.

74. **Transportation: What is the safest way to transport a cat?**

The pet carrier made of rugged plastic has long since overtaken all other travel boxes and cages, and with good reason. The carrier is very secure and offers plenty of comfort. It has a door of metal grating that closes securely and ventilation holes that let in fresh air without drafts. It is roomy, escape-proof, and easy to clean. It offers the cat protection and a view of the outside world at the same time. Especially comfortable are models with a top hatch that makes entry and exit easy. There are some disadvantages: The pet carrier is relatively large, takes up a lot of room, and is somewhat awkward to carry. Alternative ways to transport a cat:

➤ Wicker basket: Nervous cats often feel more at ease in a wicker basket than in a pet carrier, but the basket has definite drawbacks: it is heavy, very unwieldy, usually can't be securely closed, has no protection against drafts, is not escape-proof, and is hard to clean.

➤ Travel bag, made of plastic: It is lightweight and easy to carry. However, there is little room for the cat to move around in, inadequate ventilation, and no protection against escape. It is not suitable for longer trips.

➤ Transport cage, made of wire: It is used only for short trips, as it is subject to drafts and does not screen the cat from view.

➤ Carton, usually made of cardboard: These makeshift accommodations for very short trips. Can't be securely closed, has no ventilation, quickly becomes sodden.

75. Traveling: **How do I make riding in a car easier for my cat?**

Unlike dogs, cats have little enthusiasm for traveling by car. Usually only animals that got used to the car when young (see Tip, page 57) turn out to be accommodating passengers. Cats should travel only in a securely closed pet carrier, since a cat that is not confined can easily harm itself and the humans in the car, causing injuries and accidents. This applies even for supposedly calm, quiet cats such as Persians.

The ideal car is a station wagon, in the back of which the cat carrier can ride safely. Here, as on the back seat of a sedan, the carrier should be firmly secured with a belt or strap. Newspaper on the bottom of the carrier will protect the upholstery in case the cat's stomach rebels. Keep windows closed to prevent drafts, and don't point the air diffusers straight at the cat. Since a cat's body temperature is higher than ours, don't set the air conditioner too low in summer. Feed your pet no more than four hours before departure, and stop for a break after three hours at most and give the cat water to drink. On long trips, take along the litter box, and let the cat relieve itself outside only if it is on the leash. Pills to prevent travel sickness (from the vet) will help, if a cat gets overexcited during a trip, but don't make a habit of using them. Don't leave your cat in a car on a warm day.

76. Traveling: **What regulations apply to taking cats on the train or by air?**

Cats must be securely housed in a travel bag or pet carrier. For air travel, different airlines have different rates and travel regulations. Basically, the cat can be taken into the cabin as carry-on baggage, assuming here too that it is in a suitable (and waterproof) cat travel bag. Since only a certain number of animals are allowed in the cabin, you should make your flight reservation as early as possible. For detailed information, contact the individual airlines. A valid rabies vaccination is required.

INFO

Ready for love: a difficult time
If the female is not mated, she will remain in heat for up to 3 weeks. She will be restless, seek affection, roll on the floor, and try to get out to find a male cat. During the critical phase, which lasts about 7 days, she whines and yowls constantly. A lovesick tom will take every opportunity to run off, returning home from fights with his rivals covered with scratches and bites. Only neutering can offer a solution (see Info, page 148).

77. Two cats: What are the advantages of keeping two cats?

Two cats in the house are the best insurance against boredom and actually should be a requirement for all cat owners who are employed full-time and must leave their pets alone for more than 4 or 5 hours a day. Two littermates that have grown up together will be bosom buddies. If a second cat is added later, sometimes there are a few initial difficulties, but at some point the cats will get it together, become playmates, wash each other's coats, and snuggle in the cat basket. Their new life together will not impair the bond to their human; the cats' owner will continue to rank first. Now you need to buy everything in twos, as each cat has a right to its own personal things. These include a place to sleep, a food bowl, and a litter box. Separate litter boxes are important, should they wish to use the box at the same time. The scratching post is joint property, but the cats should have several places to rest and hide. Some cats are possessive about their toys, and usually each one will guard its favorite toy jealously.

78. Vacation: Who will look after our cat while we're on vacation?

With the right care, the cat is best off staying in its customary environment while you're away on vacation:
➤ Acquaintances and friends: usually familiar with the home and the cat, but they may have to make a long trip.
➤ Neighbors: can look in several times a day to see to your pet, but may lack experience with cats.
➤ House sitter: takes care of the residence and the pets, but usually lacks the time to lavish attention on your cat.
➤ Cat sitter: has the right touch for the cat and will also play and cuddle with it.
Care away from home: animal shelter (only limited room), pet boarding facility, possibly breeder (purebred cats).

Healthy Diet

The cat is a carnivore but not exclusively. In this chapter, you'll learn how to ensure that your pet has a balanced diet, avoid mistakes in feeding, prevent deficiency symptoms, and deal with problem eaters and cats that refuse to eat at all.

79. **Change in food:** Is it a good idea to switch food brands and varieties periodically?

As soon as a young cat can eat on its own, you should provide a variety of foods. Eating habits and preferences develop quite early and often last throughout a cat's life. A change in food that a kitten copes with easily is often a cause for bitter resistance in an adult cat. Quite a number of cats will refuse the new food so doggedly that their owner finally caves in. Even with store-bought food, focusing on a single brand or variety is not a good idea. Problems arise if the manufacturer discontinues production of the preferred flavor, for example, or if the cat is being boarded and has to take potluck with other food mixes, or if it has to go on a special diet. In addition, if you change the food regularly, incompatibilities are less likely to occur.

80. **Commercial cat food:** What are the advantages of feeding my cat a store-bought pet food?

➤ Good commercial cat food contains all the necessary nutrients, vitamins, and minerals.
➤ It is produced under sterile conditions and on the basis of scientific research on feline nutrition, and it is constantly quality tested.
➤ Special manufacturing procedures preserve the effectiveness of vitamins and minerals.
➤ Meat and by-products are of carefully controlled origin; high-risk organs (nerve tissue, brain, bone marrow) are not used.
➤ Both moist and dry foods can be stored and easily divided into portions.
➤ Commercial cat food makes the use of vitamin and mineral supplements unnecessary.

81. **Commercial cat food:** What does the manufacturer's label tell me?

From the label on the can or package, you can glean this information:

➤ Type of food: complete food or supplementary food.

➤ Guaranteed analysis (in percentages): gives the minimum content of protein and fat, the maximum content of crude fiber (roughage) and ash (minerals), and the moisture content. Only the group of ingredients is stated in each case; no details on composition and quality (significance and digestibility) are provided.

➤ Ingredients (listed in order of weight): Here the various forms of a certain ingredient can be listed separately. For example, it can say "lamb" on the can even though lamb accounts for no more than 4% of the total meat content, and the remainder may be pork.

➤ Supplements: vitamins, preservatives, dyes, antioxidants, flavorings.

➤ Expiration (freshness) date.

➤ Name and address of the pet food manufacturer or the vendor.

➤ Production reference number (batch number).

➤ The manufacturer's recommended portion size and number of servings.

82. Commercial cat food: Which makes a better sole food source, moist or dry pet food?

Both moist (canned) and dry pet foods are suitable as a cat's principal diet. They are similar in terms of their nutrient, vitamin, and mineral content. The main ingredient is a mix of various kinds of meats, combined with products of plant origin, such as grains (with dry food, the grain content is higher) and vegetables. The difference in water content is important: Canned food is 75 to 80% water, while dry food contains no more than 10% water. Moist food meets the cat's needs for liquid almost completely; with dry food, drinking water always has to be available, ideally at several places in your home. A diet of dry food results in greater urine concentration, which favors formation of urinary stones. In a cat this can cause a life-threatening blockage of the urethra. The advantage of dry food: The coarse pellets actively scrape off dental calculus and massage the gums. The buildup of plaque cannot be completely eliminated by a diet of kibble, however, since the predisposition to this is genetically based.

Dry kibble, in comparison to canned food, has a markedly higher energy content, which must be taken into account in determining the cat's food rations. It has a long shelf life, even after it is opened, and is extremely easy to measure out. No vitamin and mineral supplements are needed with either dry or moist food. In choosing a product, give preference to a premium pet food: It contains a higher percentage of meat than a standard brand, and the very high-quality ingredients guarantee easy digestibility. It also allows you to serve smaller portions, so that feeding your cat premium food is no more costly on balance than using a standard variety.

83. Commercial cat food: What raw materials does a good store-bought pet food contain? **?**

EXTRA TIP

A "nose" for food
Cats are picky eaters. What doesn't please them, they leave, even if they're really hungry. The smell, especially the fatty odor of meat, determines whether the meal is accepted. For this reason, the cat's food must always be at least at room temperature. Even finicky eaters can be tempted with a warm meal (about 98° (37°C)).

The origin and quality of the food's ingredients are constantly monitored in the production facilities of pet food manufacturers. Meat comes only from animals that are also approved for human consumption. Scraps from slaughtered animals, meat and/or bone meal, and high-risk organs are not processed. Good commercial cat food consists primarily of high-quality muscle meat. The "animal by-products" mentioned on the label include meat that is less easily digestible (such as intestines, lungs, meat with connective tissue). The law does not require manufacturers to list the by-products, but unless they are given on the label, there is no way for you to get an exact idea of the components. The plant-based portion (grain and vegetables) of the food should total about 30%. Important here is high-quality fat (about 10%) of animal (such as fish oil) or plant (such as sunflower oil, linseed) origin. In addition, percentages of entrails, eggs, and milk products may be present. Vitamins and minerals are specific to the animal's nutritional needs. Antioxidants are added to kibble to prevent the fat from becoming rancid. Make sure that these are natural antioxidants (vitamins E and C). Artificial antioxidants are suspected of causing allergies and can lead to liver damage and cancer.

84. **Dietary fiber: Why does a carnivore like the cat need dietary fiber?**

A cat needs more protein than other household pets and meets this requirement primarily by eating meat. Cats are not pure carnivores, however, and can't live on a diet of meat alone. Cat food must contain a certain percentage of roughage, as do the bodies of the cat's natural prey, whose bones, tendons, hair, and stomach contents it consumes. Dietary fiber is that portion of plant-based foods that cannot be completely broken down by the digestive enzymes in the

INFO

Vitamins and minerals
Vitamins and minerals are essential, even though the organism requires them only in small amounts. The cat's body can store fat-soluble vitamins (A, D, E, K), which ensure disturbance-free growth and healthy bones. Water-soluble vitamins (B-complex) must be in the diet. Vitamin C is produced by the cat's own organism. Of the minerals, sodium (in meat and fish), calcium, phosphorus, potassium, and magnesium are important.

intestine. It absorbs large quantities of water, and in the intestine it swells up and increases the volume of the intestinal contents, which further stimulates intestinal peristalsis. The soft mass of food is moved along more quickly and overall digestion is aided. Dietary fiber (cooked vegetables, starches like potatoes and pasta) keeps intestinal flora healthy. If roughage is absent, constipation and other digestive problems result. Reducing diets for overweight cats contain an especially high proportion of roughage.

85. **Dietary "sins": What are the most common mistakes in feeding a cat?**

➤ Raw meat: It can be contaminated with parasites, bacteria, and viruses.
➤ Diet of meat exclusively: Deficiency symptoms.
➤ Beef from an uncontrolled source (such as a rendering plant): It can transmit BSE, or mad cow disease, although it is rare in the U. S.
➤ Raw pork: It can be infected with the pathogens that cause Aujeszky's disease (pseudorabies), which is always fatal in cats.
➤ Raw egg white: It contains the substance avidin, which renders the essential vitamin biotin ineffective.
➤ Raw egg yolk: It carries danger of a salmonella infection.
➤ Bones (especially from poultry): Bone splinters can injure the walls of the stomach and intestine. Frequent eating of bones causes constipation.

A little sweetened whipped cream from an ice cream sundae does no harm. Otherwise, however, sweets are taboo for a cat.

➤ Raw fish: contains the enzyme thiaminase, which destroys vitamin B_1.

➤ Milk: It is not tolerated by many adult cats because of the lactose content.

➤ Sweets: They are unsuitable or dangerous for cats. Chocolate contains theobromine, which the organism cannot break down; there is a danger of poisoning.

➤ Dog food: It is specially formulated for the dog's organism. Because it contains far too little protein and fat for a cat, a steady diet of dog food will result in deficiency symptoms and serious illnesses.

If your cat shows little interest in its water bowl, you can entice it to drink by leaving a faucet dripping.

---

86. Dog food: Our cat loves to snack on dog food. Should I keep her from doing so?

An occasional snack of dog food is fine, but as a regular food it is unacceptable. Food mixtures formulated for dogs do not meet the cat's requirement for protein, partly because of the insufficient taurine content. In addition, dog food is too rich in carbohydrates and lacks the vitamins and minerals that a cat needs. The consequences of improper nutrition are apathetic behavior, a dull coat, skin diseases, and eye problems.

---

87. Drinking: My cat almost never goes to her water bowl. How can I get her motivated?

Many cats that are fed commercial canned cat food rarely visit their water bowl because the high water content of about 80% gives them an adequate supply. Not infrequently, however, owners are unaware how much their cat is drinking because it takes only a few swallows from time to time. Some cats quite consciously prefer other sources of water in the household and outdoors and leave their bowl strictly alone. Often they dislike fresh tap water because it contains too much chlorine. With a few drops of canned milk for kittens, you can make the water taste better. Coax your kitty to drink by putting bowls of water in several places in your home. Adequate fluid intake is especially important with a diet of dry food, especially for male cats, but also for older animals whose sense of thirst has diminished. The water bowl should be at least 6.5 feet (2 m) away from the food bowl.

88. Dry food: Is it all right to keep some dry food in my cat's bowl at all times?

That depends primarily on your cat's eating habits. Some cats are decidedly self-restrained, never eat more than they need, and take only a few bites on each trip to the bowl. The kibble will do them no harm. Leave the food bowl empty between meals, however, if your cat has made eating its chief occupation for lack of other activities. Otherwise, its trim figure will be threatened by the high caloric content of dry food. This applies especially to indoor cats, but it also holds true for multiple cats if one of them is envious of another's food.

89. Eating grass: Why do cats nibble on grass and other green plants?

Green plants help cats with stomach problems. At least, after nibbling on grass, sage, sedge, thyme, or parsley, it is easier for them to bring up foreign bodies, hairballs, or indigestible food components. Usually only the tender tips of grasses are consumed. It is not impossible that a cat ingests, along with the greens, vitamins such as folic acid, part of the B-complex. Little containers of cat grass (specialty stores), once they have been watered, will yield fresh grass within a few day. Grass or other suitable plants should be present in every household with a cat, even if the cats go outdoors and can find their own supply there. Cat grass also keeps your kitty from paying too much attention to your house plants.

90. **Eggs:** Is it all right to add an egg to my cat's food now and then?

Eggs provide high-quality protein and are rich in nutrients and vitamins. Once a week, it's fine to offer your cat a hard-boiled egg or scrambled egg. Most cats enjoy this and digest it easily. Unsuitable, however, is raw egg white, since it contains a substance called avidin that acts to destroy biotin and thus can produce deficiency symptoms. Biotin is one of the water-soluble vitamins of the so-called B-complex, of which a cat needs up to four times as much as a dog, for example. Undersupply of biotin makes the coat less glossy, causes hair loss, and increases susceptibility to infection. Raw egg yolk does not entail this risk, but since salmonella can be transmitted by raw egg yolk, you should make it a rule never to feed your cat raw eggs.

EXTRA TIP

Starting a diet

The special diet supports the treatment of metabolic disorders and organic damage. To rule out the possibility of malnutrition, put your pet on such a dietary regimen only if prescribed by the vet. Since diet food is usually low in fat, many cats will not accept an abrupt change of food. Mix the customary food and the diet product in a 2:1 ratio, and increase the share of diet food by 10% daily. Commercial diet foods for pets are available from the veterinarian and in specialty stores.

91. Extra food: When does a cat need larger food rations or supplementary food?

Only rarely does a cat require additional food—but never because it goes outdoors and its owner thinks it consumes more energy than an indoor cat. Only nursing mothers need more nutrients: for large litters, up to three or four times the normal amount. During pregnancy, however, the amount needed is only slightly greater. Food for young kittens, too, contains everything they need, and supplementary vitamins and minerals are neither necessary nor advisable. If your cat is ill or has deficiency symptoms, the vet will decide what changes have to be made in its diet.

THE RIGHT CAT FOOD

TYPE OF FOOD	DESCRIPTION
Moist (canned) food	Mix of various kinds of meats, plus plant-based proteins. Suitable as sole source of food. Moisture content: 75–80%.
Dry food (kibble)	Same ingredients as moist food, but higher grain content. Sole source of food. Moisture content: reduced to 10%.
Supplements	If you use store-bought pet food, no supplements are necessary. Consult with the veterinarian before adding vitamin and minerals.
Treats	Only low-calorie, high-fiber, and not on a regular basis. Suitable: snacks that promote healthy teeth.
Diet foods	Only if prescribed by the vet. Commercial diet foods are available for cats with urinary stones, liver problems, kidney problems, and other ailments.

DANGEROUS FOR CATS

Bones: splinters injure stomach and intestines; raw egg white: destroys vitamin biotin; chocolate: poisonous.

92. Fasting: Is it all right to prescribe a day of fasting for overweight cats?

Although cats are less troubled by overweight than dogs, there do exist pudgy felines that need to slim down again. For fat dogs, a day of fasting may be quite sensible and likely to get results, but for cats a starvation diet is inappropriate and harmful. The 50% method (eat half as much) does not work with a cat, since it will vigorously protest the slender helping in its food bowl. More apt to succeed: enriching the reduced food ration with dietary fiber such as vegetables or rice and thus stretching it to the customary amount. More practical and balanced than home-prepared mixtures are the specially formulated diet foods that are commercially available. These products are high in roughage and lower in calories and fat, and they can also be used as a complete food for your pet.

93. Fat content: Until now I've given my cat only lean meat. Is that wrong?

Cats need a lot of fat, in relative terms, and they also tolerate large amounts of it, distinctly more than a human. Cat food should contain at least 9% fat, with the quality of the fats being of primary importance, though fats of animal and vegetable origins must also be in the correct proportion. In the feline metabolism, fats play an important role in the absorption of vitamins A, D, E, and K. Insufficient fat leads eventually to skin and coat problems. The fat percentage also influences the taste and thus ensures the cat's acceptance of its food.

94. Feeding: Should I cut meat into little pieces before feeding it to my cat?

Cats have the teeth of a predator. Typical are the long eyeteeth or "fangs," with which the prey is seized and killed, and the so-called carnassial teeth that slice the prey into pieces. These include the last premolar in the upper jaw and the molar in the lower jaw. With them, the cat can even slice off large pieces of meat and break smaller bones. Teeth that can deal with mice and rats have no need for meals precut into morsels. Biting off the meat keeps teeth and gums fit. Further, working on larger pieces of meat provides more diversion at mealtime than the monotonous swallowing of bite-size pieces. Vigorous chewing and biting are especially important during the teething phase. By offering a young cat nothing but soft food at this stage because you want to spare it discomfort, you're doing it no favor. Usually only elderly cats with some missing teeth have a need for soft food.

95. Feeding: Kidneys are my Somali's favorite food. Should I let her have her way?

Naturally, kidney can be on your cat's menu from time to time, but it should never be the only food she eats. The meat portion of cat food must consist primarily of muscle meat, which supplies the animal's body with high-quality protein. Besides meat, ingredients of vegetable origin are important. Since kidneys are not always free of harmful substances, they must be well soaked before cooking. By serving your pet's favorite menu often, you're training it to be fixated on a certain food. Problems at home are not the only result: there will be difficulties if the cat has to stay in a boarding facility or has to adjust to a special-formula diet. And if the manufacturer changes the recipe for the cat's preferred variety, your pet may even be fussy about other commercial cat food.

96. Feeding: My male cat, at the age of 4 months, is growing fast, so I give him plenty to eat. Is this all right?

Young cats have a higher energy requirement than adult animals. Commercial kitten food is designed to meet this need with especially high-quality, energy-rich ingredients. Since a kitten's tiny stomach can deal only with tiny portions, kittens must be fed several times a day (see Feeding Plan, page 81). You need have no misgivings about putting as much food in the bowl as the little creatures can eat. At this age they are in no danger of getting fat, and when the growth phase is over, their appetite will regulate itself. In addition to monitoring the kitten's nutritional state, you also should check its weight regularly (see Info, page 91). Here the absolute body weight matters less than continual weight gain. From the time it is weaned until the sixth month, a cat should gain

FEEDING PLAN

AGE	MEALS/ DAY	TYPE OF FOOD	ENERGY REQUIREMENT, Btu/lb (kJ/kg)
Up to 8 weeks	6	Kitten food	10,500–13,000 (1.000–1.200)
Up to 3 months	5	Kitten food	9,000 (830)
From 5 months on	3	Kitten food	6,750 (625)
8–12 months	3–2	Adult food	5,400 (500)
Up to 8 years	2	Adult food	3,250–3,800 (300–350)
8 years and older	3–4	Adult food	3,700–4,100 (340–375)

DAILY REQUIREMENTS OF AN ADULT CAT

Energy requirement at a body weight of 7 pounds (3 kg), about 215 calories (900 kJ); 9 pounds (4 kg), about 285 calories (1,200 kJ); 11 pounds (5 kg), about 360 calories (1,500 kJ). A 14-ounce (400-g) can of cat food contains about 1,200 kJ, while dry food contains about 360 calories (1,500 kJ) per 3.5 ounces (100 g).

PREGNANT AND NURSING CATS

The energy requirement of a pregnant cat is only slightly higher, but nursing females need three to four times as much energy.

around 3.5 ounces (100 g) per week. A male weighs about 2–3 pounds (950–1,800 g) at the age of 4 months; at 6 months he should weigh 3.5–6 pounds (1,600–2,700 g); at 9 months, 4.5–8 pounds (2,000–3,600 g); and at the age of one year, between 5 and 9 pounds (2,300 and 4,000 g). Females weigh somewhat less.

97. Feeding rules: What's the right way to feed my cat?

➤ Fixed feeding times: if at all possible, always feed the cat at the same times.

➤ Zone with light traffic: Put the food bowl in a quiet corner (and never next to the litter box).

➤ Undisturbed: The cat wants to eat in peace and quiet.

➤ Bowl of its own: Each cat has its own food dish, and cats that are envious of each other's meals are fed separately.

➤ Always in the bowl: The food should always be served in the bowl; hand-feed your pet only in exceptional cases (see Tip below).

➤ Slightly warmed: Cat food should always be at room temperature; never serve food straight from the refrigerator.

➤ Not from the table: Human food is taboo. Feeding your cat at the table trains it to beg.

➤ Never raw: Raw meat can contain pathogens.

➤ No bones: Bones can splinter and cause internal injuries, as well as constipation.

➤ Always fresh: Partly thawed, crusted, seasoned, and smoked foods are not for cats.

➤ No dog food: Dog food cannot supply the high protein content that cats require.

➤ End of the meal: Remove leftovers after no more than 40 minutes.

➤ Put a lid on it: Once a can has been opened, cover it with a plastic lid (specialty stores) and keep the food fresh in the refrigerator.

➤ Clean dishes: Wash the food bowl with hot water (no detergent) after the meal.

➤ Fresh water: Replace drinking water at least once a day. Keep the water bowl accessible at all times.
➤ Nap: After eating, the cat needs to rest.

98. Feeding time: What's the best time of day to feed my cat?

An adult cat should be fed twice a day, in the morning and the late afternoon. If you have the time, there is no reason not to have a third mealtime at midday. That is a good idea for senior cats in particular because their digestion is no longer so efficient and small meals help the process along. Divide up the daily ration accordingly. By nature, a cat tends to be satisfied with smallish portions on its trips to the bowl anyway, but it may eat up to ten times over the course of the day. You can use mealtimes to train an indoor-outdoor cat to come home promptly: Before stalking, there's no food, but at the agreed-upon feeding time, your pet's empty stomach will automatically start complaining, and the returning roamer will be standing next to its bowl right on the dot. Cats show little understanding, however, for delayed or overlooked feeding times. Young animals must be fed several times a day because of their tiny stomachs, and the frequency depends on their age (see Feeding Plan, page 81).

99. Fish: Is fish healthy for a cat?

Many cats are crazy about fish, and there is nothing to object to in that. Fish is rich in protein, fatty acids, vitamins, and minerals. Only raw fish does not belong in the kitty's bowl: Raw fish contains the enzyme thiaminase, which breaks down and destroys vitamin B_1 in the cat's body. For this reason, fish must always be cooked before you feed it to your pet. Canned fish, such as tuna, mackerel, or sardines, should be served to the cat only occasionally and in small quantities, since it generally is quite high in fat.

100. Food allergy: Do cats have an allergic reaction to certain foods?

Cats too can suffer from inability to tolerate certain foods. For example, they may be allergic to fish or poultry, but also to ingredients of vegetable origin. Depending on the nature and severity of the allergy, diseases of the coat and skin (hair loss, edema, eczema), vomiting, or coughing fits can result. Administering antihistamines can help, but in the long run the only remedy is to eliminate the allergen. To track it down, feed the cat an "exclusion" diet, reducing its food to as few ingredients as possible. If no allergic reaction ensues, gradually add additional components to the food again. The veterinarian will give you recipes for the exclusion diet and the subsequent allergy diet.

101. Food bowl: Can I let my two Birmans eat out of the same bowl, or should each cat have its own?

Kittens do everything together and eat peaceably out of the same bowl. Among littermates, a good attitude and shared mealtimes often continue for a lifetime. Nevertheless, each cat has a right to its own food dish. This prevents quarreling, each animal is undisturbed, and you can check to see how much each one is eating. Cats that are envious of each other's food should be fed in separate rooms. Splurge on real cat food bowls; don't just use discarded ones from your own inventory of dishes. A cat is quick to notice that the meals are served only in its own personal bowl, and then it is less apt to think of snitching food from other plates. Moreover, a good cat bowl is sturdy and skid-proof. Usually it has a rubber ring that keeps the cat from pushing it all over the kitchen floor when it eats.

102. Food quantity: Do I always have to follow the recommended amounts?

The feeding recommendations on the packaging are based on data obtained by the manufacturer in feeding tests with cats of average weight (about 9–11 pounds (4–5 kg)) and average size and activity level. The recommendations for standard complete foods usually are somewhat too high. Start with 10% less and check over a period of several days to see whether your cat is full. The food requirement depends largely on physical activity (stay-at-home or indoor-outdoor cat), the season (less food in hot weather), special circumstances (loss of appetite in a female in heat), and, not least of all, the variations in the metabolizing of the nutrients in the cat's body (good and poor metabolizers). With special-formula food (for pregnant or nursing females, for example), follow the recommendations as closely as possible. This applies especially to diet food, where the veterinarian must always be consulted as well, however.

103. Forced feeding: How do I go about force-feeding my cat, if required?

This is a tried-and-true technique: Hold the cat's head from behind, and press on the corners of its jaw until it opens its mouth. Using a disposable syringe plunger (minus the needle), squirt the liquid or semi-liquid food into its mouth from one side. Give it only small amounts each time, always closing your pet's mouth until it has swallowed. Talk to it in a gentle voice, and take breaks periodically.

104. Hairballs: Can hair that has been swallowed cause gastrointestinal problems?

Cats are very clean animals and groom their body and coat several times a day. The tongue is used for cleaning the coat. Along with dirt particles, it also picks up dead hairs, many of which stick to the tiny barbs on the cat's tongue and are swallowed. That can be a lot of hair, especially during molting and with longhaired cats in general. In the stomach, the hairs mix together with the soft food mass and form balls, so-called bezoars. Smaller bezoars are regurgitated with relative ease or pass out of the body through the intestine. With larger ones, the cat often has to cough them up, which is exhausting and agonizing. Frequent vomiting can lead to inflammation of the stomach lining, and in rare cases very large hairballs even have to be surgically removed. Cat grass makes bezoars easier to bring up.

A few drops of olive oil in the cat food or an anti-hairball treat (from specialty stores) will aid digestion and ensure that most of the swallowed hair is eliminated normally, as well as keep hairballs from forming at all. This is especially important with longhaired cats and breeds that shed heavily.

105. Kitten food: Until what age should young cats be fed kitten food?

Commercial canned pet food for kittens is especially high in energy and formulated for the young animals' special vitamin and mineral requirements. Use the specially designed mix until about the twelfth month. The growth phase is over by then, and the nutrient requirement is decreasing, as your pet's appetite will indicate: At this age, cats no longer eat as voraciously as they did in the first few months of life.

106. Lack of appetite: Recently my cat has been eating only half of its food. What might be causing this?

Cats are fussy when it comes to food. There are a number of things that cause them to eat less or refuse food altogether. These factors are directly related to feeding:

➤ Overfeeding. If a healthy cat regularly leaves part of the food in the bowl, cut back the serving gradually (by about 10% each time), until it is eating everything.

➤ Substandard food. The cat's organism is dependent on high-quality animal protein. Meat and fish are rich in vital amino acids. Malnourishment with substandard meat can lead to loss of appetite, a shaggy coat, emaciation, and growth disturbances.

➤ Cooked meals. Long cooking destroys important vitamins (such as A and B_1). Loss of appetite is an initial symptom of too high a percentage of cooked food in the cat's diet. Serious illnesses can result.

➤ Snacks. If the cat regularly gets snacks between meals, its appetite will necessarily diminish. Cut back on the little treats in between.

➤ Eating at the neighbor's house. If a cat goes outdoors, you can't always control what it may be fed. Ask your neighbors. Even if it is well meant, the additional feeding should be stopped. Don't forget: Cats rarely will reject dog food that is sitting out somewhere on a patio or on cellar stairs.

Other potential causes of poor appetite:

➤ Dental problems. Tooth loss and gum inflammations can cause cats to eat little or refuse food altogether (perhaps because they can no longer chew solid food).

➤ Kidney and liver diseases. Here loss of appetite is frequently an attendant symptom. If you suspect illness, get the veterinarian involved at once.

➤ Heat. A cat that is in heat (see Info, page 65) eats very little. Her appetite will return later.

➤ Summer. Like humans, cats don't feel like eating much in very hot weather.

➤ Lack of exercise. Inactive cats that won't come out of the woodwork often have a very low energy requirement. Try to interest them in games and exercise.

107. Leftover food: Is it all right to serve the cat the leftovers from its previous meal?

With dry food there is no objection to this, but with moist food you should always remove everything left in the cat's food bowl after its meal, and wash the bowl in hot water immediately. After only a few hours, canned food loses its freshness, taste, and aroma, and begins to crust. Since a cat always sniffs its food before eating, it would no longer accept the old food anyway. Besides, flies and other insects can land on the uncovered food and possibly contaminate it with disease-causing organisms. The opened can will stay fresh if you store it in the refrigerator, covered with a plastic lid (specialty stores) to remain airtight. But please take it out of the refrigerator in good time or put it briefly in the microwave, so that your cat doesn't have a cold meal.

108. Meat: Why can't cats be fed raw meat?

Raw or undercooked meat is as unsafe for your cat as it is for you. This is true regardless of whether the meat is wild-caught prey or processed for human consumption. Meats may contain all sorts of disease-causing pathogens that normally are destroyed by the high heat of cooking. You and your cat can contract the organism that causes toxoplasmosis by eating raw or undercooked meats. Salmonella bacteria is another potential threat that causes symptoms ranging from ordinary diarrhea to life-threatening systemic illness. Raw organ meats may harbor roundworm larvae or other parasites. Feeding raw fish or tuna meant for human consumption isn't good for your cat either. Raw fish and all-fish diets can cause serious vitamin deficiencies. However, the fish and tuna varieties of commercial cat foods generally contain added supplements to guarantee balanced nutrition. It is best to stick with commercial cat foods because they are cooked at high enough temperatures to destroy the pathogens and parasites that can be found in meat.

109. Mice: Our tom often catches mice. Should I reduce his food ration accordingly?

No, your cat is unlikely to catch more than three or four mice per day; even experienced hunters often come away empty-handed. A mouse is a mere palate-teaser: A cat weighing about 9 pounds (4 kg) needs 285 calories (1,200 kJ) of energy per day, while a mouse provides a maximum of 29 calories (120 kJ).

Moreover, a cat doesn't eat all the prey it catches. And since your pet can become infected with tapeworms by eating rats and mice, you should take the prey away if it is brought into the house. To compensate, give your pet a little treat.

110. Milk: Why isn't milk a good drink for cats?

Although it is rich in valuable vitamins and minerals, cow's milk is not a suitable drink for cats, whether it is fresh or boiled. Many adult cats can't digest the lactose in the milk, since they lack the proper enzyme, and they get diarrhea. Reduced-lactose milk products such as farmer cheese and yogurt, however, can be served without reservation. The cat should meet its needs for liquid by drinking water exclusively. Once in a while you can give it some diluted evaporated milk.

1 *Water is the only proper drink for a cat. Provide fresh water every day, ideally in several bowls at different locations in your home.*

2 *Now and then, a dab of cream or a tiny piece of butter are all right; otherwise, feed your cat by hand only in exceptional circumstances.*

111. Nutrition: Can a cat live on a diet of meat alone?

A cat can't live without meat, but it also can't live on meat alone. Meat, preferably muscle meat including beef, poultry, and fish, meets cats' requirements for high-quality protein. But meat lacks important fat-soluble vitamins, as well as iodine and biotin (vitamin H), which must be ingested with the food. In addition, a one-sided diet of meat results in calcium deficiency and leads to enormous skeletal problems, paralysis, and bone fractures.

112. Nutrition: Do I have to serve senior-formula foods to our 11-year-old female cat?

A cat remains fit and mobile for many years, and visible signs of old age are registered only at a late date. But even if everything appears to be fine on the outside, aging leaves its traces on internal organs. This applies especially to the stomach and intestine and to digestion of proteins and fats. Although old age affects cats in very different ways, in general a 9- or 10-year-old animal can be considered elderly. Now is the time to switch from normal food for adult cats to a special formula for senior felines. Foods made for seniors are especially easy to digest but are relatively high in calories and in line with the cat's requirements for high-quality protein. It is advisable to divide the daily ration into three meals instead of two. Older cats sometimes develop rather peculiar food preferences and are in some cases finicky eaters. Usually, little kinks can be tolerated without any compunction. Make sure the cat is allowed to eat undisturbed, give it more time at its food bowl, and check regularly to see whether it is drinking enough.

113. Nutritional condition: How can I tell whether I'm feeding my cat a balanced, healthy diet?

Indicators of proper nutrition are the cat's physical shape and behavior. A healthy cat has a good appetite.

It does not gulp its food like a dog; instead, it eats with enjoyment and frequently also takes short breaks. Some cats leave a little food in the bowl "for later," a sign that they are full and the portion was exactly right. A well-nourished cat is neither too fat nor too thin. Here's how to check: Your cat is overweight if you have to press hard on the side of its chest to feel its ribs. If the diet is well-balanced, the cat's coat is glossy, not dull or rough. The cat has good digestion and proper stool consistency.

114. Refusal of food: **Do I need to take my cat to the vet if it doesn't touch its food for over 24 hours?**

It is always an alarm signal when a cat with a previously normal appetite stops eating. The causes of loss of appetite are usually quickly identified (for example, a female in heat, feeding by neighbors, high outdoor temperatures), and usually the cat will take a few bites or accept a treat. If it refuses to eat anything at all for more than a day, however, that usually is a symptom of illness, and you absolutely should take it to the vet.

Prolonged failure to eat will result in liver damage (fatty liver) due to the excessive concentration of fatty acids. Refusal to eat can be triggered by constipation; a foreign body in the throat, stomach, or intestine; injuries in the mouth and throat areas (such as a broken jaw after a fall); hairballs that are not vomited up; and inflammations of the oral mucosa and gums. Gum inflammations are not infrequently the result of dental calculus, but they also

INFO

Is my cat's weight right?
Small, lightweight cats and young cats can be weighed in the container of kitchen or postal scales. To weigh an adult cat, hold it in your arms and step on your bathroom scales. Then weigh yourself, and subtract your weight from the first number. Regularly checking your pet's weight at 2-week intervals is an important part of preventive health care.

accompany some infectious diseases (cat AIDS, feline leukemia). Stress can also cause a cat to quit eating. Possible reasons: neglect, changes in family structure, oppression by other cats, a move, and competition from other pets. Determining the cause is not always easy; usually the eating disorder will not disappear until the situation also changes. With cats that object to a change in their diet and go on a hunger strike (see below), the reasons are more obvious.

115. Special diet: My male cat has kidney disease and has to follow a special diet. How can I help him adjust to this food?

Many cats stubbornly insist on having their customary food and categorically refuse any change in diet. With a special diet, there is also the problem that the fat content is usually lower than that of normal food. And since it is precisely the fat that makes the food taste good, the switch to diet food can cause additional problems. For the best results, change the food percentages gradually: Mix the cat's usual food in a 2:1 ratio with the diet food, and increase the share of diet food with each meal, by about 10 percent each time. Not infrequently, a cat with kidney disease must stay on a special diet the rest of its life. You need to make sure that your male cat is drinking plenty of liquid.

116. Sweets: Is it true that sweets are harmful to cats?

With the taste buds at the tip and the base of its tongue, a cat can distinguish various flavors. It can best recognize sour flavors, but bitter and salty ingredients in its food can be detected as well.

Obviously it lacks the ability to taste sweet things. This may explain why many cats have no interest at all in sweets. But there are others that enjoy nibbling on cakes, pies, or other baked goods. Even if it's usually only the allure of the forbidden that leads the cat into temptation, sweets should be off limits—especially chocolate. It contains theobromine, a substance that is not broken down by the cat's body and leads to poisoning. What is true for sweets is even truer for alcoholic beverages: Even small amounts of alcohol are harmful for cats.

117. Taurine: I read everywhere how important taurine is for cats. What does it offer?

Cat food must contain high-quality animal proteins (especially muscle meats), but also a certain percentage of plant-based proteins. Amino acids are the building blocks of proteins. Taurine is one of the eleven vital amino acids that cannot be made by the cat's own body and must be ingested in food. Taurine is supplied only by animal tissue; it is absent in foods of plant origin. Taurine deficiency leads to growth disturbances, heart damage, and eye problems to the point of blindness. Commercial cat food contains taurine in sufficient amounts.

118. Treats: How can I give my kitty some treats with a clear conscience?

Cats are real gourmets. Many enjoy yogurt, farmer cheese, cottage cheese, and similar dairy products. Because these products are lower in lactose, they are usually well tolerated, unlike cow's milk. Cats also

EXTRA TIP

Hand-feeding should be the exception
The cat has its own food bowl (not just any old plate from the cupboard), in which all meals and any treats are served. Resort to hand-feeding only with cats that are weakened by illness and nursing queens, if they refuse to leave their offspring alone in the first few days. Later, offer kittens small amounts of soft food on your fingertip to make the switch to solid foods easier.

appreciate canned fish, such as mackerel, sardines, or tuna, but they should be served only in small quantities because of their high fat content. Some cats adore oatmeal, which can simply be sprinkled over the cat food, and there is also no objection to a little piece of butter once a week. Good for teeth and gums are chewable tablets or strips, as well as snacks specially designed to promote healthy teeth.

119. Underweight: My cat eats normally, but it is underweight. Am I giving it the wrong food?

Malnutrition is one of the possible causes of underweight or weight loss. This occurs when the food fails to meet the cat's energy needs because it contains too much meat with low nutritional value (such as lung) or the percentage of hard-to-digest or indigestible plant roughage is too high. Give your pet premium commercial cat foods. With moist (canned) food, the daily requirement of a normally active cat weighing around 9 lb (4 kg) is about 11–14 ounces (320–410 g). Since senior cats are less able to digest protein and fat, older cats need a relatively high-calorie food to retain their strength. If your cat eats a balanced diet but does not gain weight, the vet should examine it. Loss of weight and conditioning with no change in appetite are typical symptoms of diabetes or of pancreatitis, as well as of infestation with roundworms or hookworms, which can affect even young kittens.

INFO

Dietary dangers
➤ **Meat:** Feeding meat exclusively leads to calcium deficiency and skeletal changes.
➤ **Raw fish:** It destroys the vitamin thiamine.
➤ **Liver:** in excess, liver causes vitamin A poisoning.
➤ **Raw egg:** It can contain salmonella.
➤ **Milk:** Many adult cats have lactose intolerance.
➤ **Dog food:** It causes deficiency symptoms.

120. Valerian: Do all cats react to the smell of valerian and catnip?

The scent of valerian and catnip (*Nepeta cataria*) attracts cats irresistibly. Many show symptoms of an ecstatic state and seem completely disconnected from reality. The reaction is triggered by essential oils like those found in the leaves and stem of catnip. These "drugs for the nose" have no negative consequences for the cat. Male cats react with special intensity. Even a few drops of valerian can be enough to make all the males in the entire neighborhood come running. Not all cats are susceptible to the intoxicating scents, however: Half of all cats couldn't care less about valerian and catnip.

121. Vegetarian food: My friend feeds her dog an almost exclusively vegetarian diet. Will that work with a cat too?

A cat needs substantially more protein and fat than a dog. It is dependent on a supply of high-quality nutrients of animal origin and cannot live as a vegetarian. A number of vital substances that the cat's body cannot produce on its own are present in food of animal origin, but not in vegetables. These include arachidonic acid and the amino acid taurine. The requirement for vitamin A (important for skin, eyes, and healthy growth) also must be met by consuming animal protein, while a dog (like a human) can produce the vitamin on its own by converting it from its carotene precursor, found in plants.

122. Vitamins: Can vitamins make my cat's coat glossier?

Dull, rough hair and brittle claws are often the result of a biotin deficiency. Biotin (vitamin H) is especially important in molting. Other B-complex vitamins (such as B_2) also ensure strong, lustrous hair and prevent dandruff and dry skin. Specially formulated food supplements for this purpose are commercially available.

123. Weaning: At what age should a kitten start eating solid food?

At the age of 3 or 4 weeks, kittens should be presented with an occasional piece of meat. They are not yet able to eat it, but they will nibble and gnaw at it, which strengthens their chewing muscles and promotes tooth formation. Starting in the fifth week, you can begin giving them solid food. After this point, the mother is increasingly less willing to let her offspring nurse whenever they're so inclined. And at this age, the young kittens are ready for new tastes, since initial food preferences often develop in this early phase. The smell of the food obviously plays a central role: The various scents will be stored in the kittens' brains permanently. Variety in the food bowl is important for cats from kittenhood on, to avoid creating problem eaters and cats that are fixated on a single food.

124. Weight problems: Can I put my overweight male cat on a half-ration diet?

Certainly, the best way to restore that dream figure is to reduce your cat's food ration. But you can't count on getting its support for this plan. It will not be happy that its bowl is only half full, and it will pester you until you give in to its complaints. It makes more sense to serve the tubby tom his normal quantity, but with a lower caloric content. Put about 60% of the usual food in his bowl, and the rest should be low-calorie roughage such as rice. If the cat rejects that

By offering a variety of foods, you keep the kittens from developing one-sided food preferences.

too, start with a 9:1 mixture of normal food and roughage, and successively increase the roughage portion over the next few weeks. Play with your tom before meals: Playing until he's tired will reduce his appetite. In any event, discuss the diet with your vet beforehand. He or she will tell you what to pay attention to and can recommend commercial diet foods that make weight reduction easier.

Health and Grooming

In this chapter, you'll find all the
information you need, as well as
plenty of practical tips, to groom
your cat properly and keep it in
good health. Early detection of illness, vaccinations, alternative
veterinary medicine, and first aid
for felines are only a few of the
topics covered.

125. Abscess: A bite on my tomcat's paw has turned into a nasty abscess. Can something like this be prevented?

Whenever toms get into a scrap, bites and scratches usually result. The front legs and paws generally get the worst of it. At first glance, the injuries may look relatively harmless, but the long, sharp eyeteeth sink deep into the tissue and leave many pathogens there. If an inflamed wound is not treated promptly, the tissue swells and an abscess, often containing a large quantity of pus, is formed. The disease process almost always affects the cat's overall well-being. It seems off-color, runs a temperature, and eats virtually nothing. The germs can also attack other organs and seriously impair your pet's heart, kidneys, and liver. Even harmless-looking bites and scratches need to be kept under careful observation. In case of doubt, take your cat to the vet as quickly as possible.

126. AIDS: How dangerous is feline AIDS? Can it be transmitted to humans?

Feline Immunodeficiency Virus (FIV) is transmitted by direct cat-to-cat contact, primarily through bites, but also during mating. The initial, as yet nonspecific, symptoms often appear only years later (loss of appetite, weight loss, fever), and they are followed by blood changes, skin diseases, inflammations of the oral and nasal cavities, and increased susceptibility to infection. Ultimately the weakening of the immune system leads to the death of the affected animal.

Acupressure can help cats too: Gentle pressure at certain points on the body is relaxing and promotes healing.

Because of its similarity to human HIV, FIV is also known as "feline AIDS." Humans are at no risk from FIV-infected cats. Vaccine is available for cats.

127. Alternative medicine: Which methods of alternative veterinary medicine are used to treat cats?

Characteristic of alternative veterinary medicine are natural remedies and gentle types of treatments. Certain methods are said to help strengthen resistance to disease, promote self-healing, and support and supplement traditional medicine. Especially with allergies, chronic pain, and conspicuous behavioral issues, therapy based on naturopathy can help improve a pet's quality of life.

➤ Homeopathy: Animal, plant, and mineral substances are used not to counteract, but to produce, symptoms of disease in order to stimulate the body's own healing processes.

➤ Acupuncture: Traditional Chinese medicine provides the basis for acupuncutre. At certain fixed acupuncture points, the energy flow is stimulated or suppressed with needles or laser pens. In gold acupuncture, particles of gold are implanted, primarily to treat joint ailments.

➤ Acupressure: Fingers are used to put slight pressure on the acupuncture points. It is helpful with cats that resist insertion of acupuncture needles.

➤ Bach flowers: In this form of therapy, flower essences from wild plants are administered to help reduce stress and alleviate behavioral problems.

➤ Phytotherapy: Concentrated mixtures of herbal medicines are used.

➤ Magnetic field therapy: Magnetic pulses are said to strengthen the immune defense system and reduce the time needed to convalesce after injuries.

➤ Aromatherapy: Aromatic substances are said to have a soothing or stimulating effect on cats and are used in specific ways as part of aromatherapy. They include balm (calming), sage (anti-inflammatory), and juniper (antispasmodic).

➤ Massage therapy: It promotes healing of diseases of the musculoskeletal system and muscle injuries.

➤ Light therapy: Depending on the clinical picture, the cat is exposed to light of different wavelengths, especially red light. Red light combats nervousness and anxiety and provides soothing warmth.

➤ Tellington Touch: Originally developed for training horses, Tellington Touch now is used with various animals, even cats. Making circular movements, the therapist's fingers massage individual spots on the body to promote relaxation and concentration and strengthen the bond between pet and owner.

128. Anal sacs: How do the anal sacs become impacted?

The two anal glands located to the right and left of the anus produce secretions that collect in the anal sacs and normally are discharged regularly along with the stool. Lack of cleanliness, as well as a genetic predisposition, can lead to impacted anal sacs, a condition accompanied by itching and pain. Frequently the cat seeks relief by dragging its hindquarters across the floor ("sledding," also typical of worm infestation). To prevent inflammation, the clogged anal sacs must be emptied immediately. That should always be left to the veterinarian, who has the necessary experience and expertise to spare the cat pain during this procedure.

129. Anus: What can possibly cause my cat's anal area to be dirty all the time?

A healthy cat does not neglect its anal area during its daily grooming. An anal region that is constantly sticky and soiled, therefore, is always a sign that something is wrong. For longhaired cats with an especially dense coat, the explanation is obvious: The cleaning efforts alone are not enough to keep the hairy anal area clean. To remedy the situation, clip the coat all around the anus. In senior cats, mobility sometimes decreases considerably, and when washing themselves they are no longer able to reach every body part. In this case, help is needed. This applies especially to seniors that are affected by arthrosis (degenerative changes in a joint, often near the spinal column). The cards are also stacked against the overweight cat, whose own abdomen gets in their way, and soon they stop trying to clean their bottom. Diarrhea, however, also leaves the anal area sticky with feces. Diarrhea is an indication of impaired health, even of serious disease, depending on the other symptoms.

130. Arthrosis: What increases susceptibility to arthrosis?

Arthrosis is the term applied to degenerative changes in joints. In cats, such signs of wear and tear appear primarily in old age. Almost 20% of elderly cats suffer from arthrosis, which frequently affects the spinal column. Various things can result in joint damage: weak ligaments, overuse, an awkward position of the legs, obesity, osteoporosis, and hormonal imbalances, as well as improper nutrition, allergies, and genetic predisposition. The wear and tear on the joint cartilage not infrequently leads to inflammation of the articular cartilage lining the joint (arthritis). Arthritis causes the cat such great pain that it is forced to limp, trying to reduce the stress on the affected leg. Arthro-

INFO

What your vet needs to know
This information will make the diagnosis easier for your vet:
➤ General symptoms: How long has the cat had these problems? Has its condition worsened in the past few hours? Is it vomiting, does it have diarrhea, or is there blood in its urine?
➤ Appetite: What did it eat last? Has it possibly ingested poisons (chemicals, poisonous plants)?
➤ Behavior: Is it apathetic, restless, or aggressive?
➤ Medicine: Has it just been given any medications?

sis cannot be cured; its course can only be moderated. Warmth is helpful. The vet can prescribe tablets, but joint injections usually give only brief relief. The life of old cats suffering from arthrosis or rheumatism can be made easier with climbing aids and little stairs, to give them better access to favorite places.

131. Assisting at the birth: When does a queen need help in delivering her kittens?

Only rarely does a human have to jump in and act as a midwife for a cat. Most queens know exactly what to do when. You should give the mother cat support in these cases:

➤ Amniotic sac: The mother licks her young clean right after birth. If there are nonetheless remnants of the amniotic sac on a newborn kitten, you can use your fingers to remove them carefully.

➤ Umbilical cord: Most queens sever the umbilical cord without needing any help. But if it ever is forgotten in the excitement (with a first litter, perhaps), you can cut through the cord with scissors. Cut it off about 1 inch (3 cm) from the kitten's body, and then press the sides of the stub together to stop the bleeding.

➤ Taking a breath: If a newborn kitten is not breathing, there is amniotic fluid in its lungs. Take the kitten in your hand, its head pointing outwards, and quickly turn its body in circles until the water is gone.

➤ Reviving: If a newborn is cool to the touch and is not moving, a warm bath for 3 or 4 minutes will help. Massage its body gently in the water, making sure its head stays above water. Dry the kitten well.

➤ Massage: Newborn kittens can relieve themselves only if the queen licks their abdomen and anus. If she neglects to do this, you need to stimulate the digestive process by gently rubbing the lower abdomen.

➤ Clean and warm: Giving birth is a damp business for cats. Replace the wet cloths and soaked newspapers as soon as possible. If the damp deprives the young of the warmth they need, life-endangering hypothermia will develop within a short time.

➤ Help from the vet: Call the veterinarian if no kitten has been born after 2 hours of labor, if the labor pains stop for more than an hour although not all the kittens have been born, and if the mother is so exhausted that she no longer can push.

132. Bad breath: If my cat has bad breath, does that have anything to do with its food?

Bad breath can have a dietary origin only if you constantly serve your cat a lot of fish. If that is the case, halitosis would not be the worst of it: Fish contains too little calcium, iron, and vitamin A, and a diet of fish alone would soon lead to deficiency symptoms and diseases. If the cat has bad breath, that generally indicates that its oral mucosa are inflamed or that it is suffering from tartar buildup. Halitosis is also a symptom of kidney diseases. If there are problems in the mouth and throat area, a foul odor will come from the cat's mouth, but if there is kidney inflammation, the odor tends to be sweetish. In any event, the cause must be determined by the vet.

133. Bathing: When does a cat need a bath?

Cats need to bathe only if their coat is so dirty that they can't clean it on their own, if they were in contact with toxic substances, if they are infested with parasites, or if they have certain skin and coat diseases. Here's how to bathe even an unwilling pet: Fill a sink or small tub about 4 inches (10 cm) deep with lukewarm water, put the cat in it (ideally, on a skidproof mat), dampen its coat, and apply a special pet shampoo labeled as safe for cats or the cleanser prescribed by your vet. When you're done, rinse out the shampoo carefully and dry the cat with a hand towel (no blow drying). Its face should be cleaned only with a damp cloth. After the bath, the cat has to stay indoors until its skin and coat are completely dry. Animals that stubbornly resist the tub can be cleaned with a dry shampoo for cats, which is rubbed into the coat. Dry bathing, however, cleans only a lightly soiled coat and is less suitable for longhaired cats because, in their case, the active agent is hard to brush out completely. Medicinal baths are called for only if recommended by the vet. A cat's eyes, ears, mouth, and nose should not come into contact with the lotion.

134. Birth: **What is the normal process of giving birth for a cat?**

Usually there are three to six, sometimes even eight, young, which are born after a gestation period of 63 days (for some breeds, only 60 days). Delivering a large number of offspring is an exhausting business, but since the cat's body is constituted for bearing many young, problems rarely occur at all, and if they do then they are usually in a few purebred breeds or in first-time mothers. Although every feline mother-to-be behaves differently, most appreciate having their owner nearby during the delivery.

➤ Restlessness before parturition: In the hours before delivery, the cat becomes very restive and wanders around the house aimlessly. She will not eat at this time, but drinking water should be available.

➤ Initial labor pains: With the onset of labor, the cat will seek out the birthing box.

➤ Delivery: Immediately before giving birth, the bubble-like amniotic sac becomes visible. The cat

INFO

Vaccination schedule
At the time of vaccination, a cat must be healthy and free of worms. Basic immunizations (first series of shots): are rhino-tracheitis, calici virus, and feline distemper (panleukopenia), weeks 8–9 and 12–13; rabies, weeks 12–14; feline leukemia virus, weeks 16–20 and 20–24; FIP, weeks 16–20 and 20–24. Vaccination against FIP (feline infectious peritonitis) is not recommended by all veterinarians. Booster shots are required annually. Even animals that never go outdoors should be vaccinated against rabies. Rabies vaccinations are required by law in most areas.

frees each newborn from the sac by using her teeth and tongue, and bites through the umbilical cord. Most queens eat the placenta, which either is still connected to the kitten or is expelled later.

➤ Duration: The process may be over in just 1 hour, but it also can take 6 or 7 hours. If numerous young are born and some take up to 2 hours, the mother has to use her last reserves of strength, and afterward she needs plenty of rest in order to recover.

135. **Bronchitis:** **From time to time my tomcat suffers from coughing fits, but otherwise he's healthy. What triggers the coughing?**

If a cat coughs now and then, there's no cause for concern. It may have swallowed the wrong way, or breathed in something that it removes from its respiratory passages by coughing. Prolonged or persistent coughing fits, however, must be taken seriously. In most cases, a respiratory infection is the cause, but the need to cough can also be triggered by allergic reactions.

Inflammations in the nose and throat area not infrequently lead to bronchitis. With an acute inflammation of the bronchial tubes, a cat has fever and suffers from violent coughing fits, accompanied by production of mucus and pus. The vet will prescribe medications to lower the fever and loosen the mucus. If not treated in time, bronchitis can lead to pneumonia. Chronic bronchitis is one of the most common respiratory diseases of elderly cats. Typical are the agonizing coughing fits that cause the animals a great deal of discomfort, while the rest of the time they usually have no complaints. Generally the disease requires prolonged treatment with antibiotics.

136. **Car accident:** **What do I do if a cat has been hit by a car?**

Road traffic is the biggest source of danger for cats that go outdoors. If a cat is hit by a car, security must first be provided for the accident site, as with any

CARE SCHEDULE

Daily	➤ Eyes: Dab off secretions and tears with a piece of absorbent cotton that has been dampened with lukewarm water. ➤ Paws: Check for cracks and wounds. Wash off dirty areas (road salt, tar) and remove foreign bodies between the toes (thorns, tiny stones) with tweezers. ➤ Coat care for longhaired cats: Smooth matted coat areas with wide-tooth comb, loosen knots in coat by hand, remove dirt with small-tooth comb, go over coat again with wire- and natural-bristle brush. For semi-longhaired cats, grooming is needed only every other day. ➤ Skin: When grooming coat, check for injuries, changes, and parasites.
Weekly	➤ Teeth: Any coatings or foreign bodies? Gums: Are they reddened? Possibly clean with toothbrush. There are specially formulated snacks to promote dental hygiene. ➤ Ears: Clean ear flaps with cotton and baby oil. Don't use cotton swabs. Brown crusts and unpleasant smell are indications of ear mites. Treatment by vet only. ➤ Anus: Clean dirty or sticky areas with soft cloth and lukewarm water. Trim hair if it is always stuck together. ➤ Claw check: Is there normal wear and tear, or are they splintered or broken? ➤ Coat care for shorthaired cat: Use small-tooth comb to remove dead hair, dirt, and possibly parasites; then go over again using brush with molded rubber teeth. The natural-bristle brush helps the circulation.
Annually	Booster shots and "big check-up" by the vet.
As needed	➤ Stomach and intestine: Anti-hairball product (found in specialty stores) and malt paste regulate digestion. Cat grass must be available at all times. ➤ Bathing: Bathe cat if it is very dirty, if there has been contact with poison, or if directed by the vet. ➤ Massage: It promotes good circulation. ➤ Worming: Worm as recommended by vet.

other traffic accident. Then move the injured animal as quickly as possible out of the danger area. Before the trip to the vet, lifesaving measures are often necessary if, for example, the cat is unconscious, in shock, bleeding heavily, or not breathing (see First Aid, page 118). Gentle handling is important, especially with unclear symptoms (suspicion of internal injuries), broken bones, or a spinal injury. Phone the vet before you get in the car, or contact the nearest animal hospital if your vet can't be reached. Don't forget to have someone tell you the fastest way to get there so that you don't lose a single minute.

137. Care: What is important in taking care of a sick cat?

➤ Above all, peace and quiet: Sick animals need lots of sleep and should not be disturbed, if at all possible. Put the cat's bed in a quiet corner, or set aside a room for use as the cat's sickroom.
➤ Warmth is beneficial: Put the sickbed near the radiator. Cats that have just had surgery or anesthesia should be covered with a blanket to prevent hypothermia. Red light is helpful with respiratory diseases.
➤ Drink plenty of water: An adequate supply of drinking water is especially important for a sick cat. The water bowl has to be easily accessible.

INFO

The healthy cat at a glance
➤ Abdomen and flanks are neither sunken nor swollen.
➤ Coat is not matted and has no bare spots or defects.
➤ Eyes are clear, nose is dry and warm, and ears are clean.
➤ Teeth have no tartar buildup, and mucous membranes and gums are pink.
➤ Anus is not dirty; feces and urine are not discolored.
➤ Pads of feet are not cracked; claws are not broken.
➤ Cat has no problems with walking, jumping, and climbing.
➤ Animal is alert, enjoys contact, and has normal appetite.

➤ Hand-feeding: Feed debilitated cats by offering small bits of food in the palm of your hand or putting soft food on your fingertip. In an emergency, the cat must be force-fed.

➤ Tablets and drops.

➤ Giving injections: A diabetic cat must be injected with insulin daily. To do so, gently pull up the skin at the back of your pet's neck and insert the needle beneath the skin. Change the injection site regularly.

➤ Changing a dressing: After removing the old bandage, use absorbent cotton soaked in disinfectant to dab the wound if there is any discharge. Then dust on a dressing powder for wounds, apply a piece of gauze, and wrap the affected area in an elastic bandage.

138. Cystitis: Our cat urinates very frequently. What is causing this?

A constant urge to urinate is an indication of an inflammation of the bladder or feline lower urinary tract disorder (FLUTD), which usually is caused by bacteria. Renal gravel and bladder stones promote infection, as they often damage the bladder wall, which makes it easier for germs to multiply. A cat with cystitis tries to urinate at short intervals. It strains, but can release only a little urine each time and often finds the process painful. The urine usually looks normal, but it may be discolored or contain blood, if gravel or stones have injured the bladder lining. The vet will treat the problem with antibiotics.

Changes in your cat's litter box behavior can frequently be traced to a disease of the bladder or the kidneys.

139. Deafness: Why are almost all pure-white cats with blue eyes deaf?

The inner ear (labyrinth) of blue-eyed white cats is almost always impaired, which results in hearing difficulties or deafness. The white coat coloration of these animals is caused by a dominant gene (W gene). This form of deafness is congenital and inheritable. The young of blue-eyed cats with normal hearing ability may also be deaf. More rarely, white cats with other eye colors have hearing loss. Deafness leads to considerable behavioral deficits: Deaf cats hunt by sight, since they cannot locate their prey acoustically. Communicating with other cats is problematic because warning and threatening sounds go unheard. Deaf mother cats do not react to the whimpers of their young when they cry for help. In odd-eyed cats, hearing loss affects only the ear on the blue-eyed side. Here the direction-finding sense is impaired, and the cat cannot determine where noises are coming from.

140. Diabetes: Can diabetic cats lead a life free of complaints?

In feline diabetes, the sugar contained in food cannot be properly used because the pancreas no longer produces the hormone insulin, which is needed for this purpose. Symptoms of illness are an increase in appetite accompanied by weight loss and excessive thirst. Usually the coat, too, is in poor condition.

Older and obese cats are especially susceptible to diabetes. As with humans, the missing insulin must be supplied through daily injection. To decide on the right dose, the vet will determine the blood sugar level beforehand, and this test will be repeated at regular intervals. If the sugar levels are right, the cat can lead a complaint-free life, with minor restrictions. For example, it must have its injection at fixed times, if at all possible, and not be out hunting somewhere and thus unavailable. Taking care of a diabetic cat inevitably restricts its owner's freedom of movement, and since there is no cure for diabetes, this often remains true for many years.

141. Diarrhea: My male Siamese has diarrhea now and then, but it never lasts long. Do I need to do something about it?

Diarrhea, like vomiting, is a sign that the cat doesn't feel well. There may be many reasons for this, ranging from rather harmless gas, allergic reactions, or spoiled food all the way to chronic gastrointestinal inflammations, infections, diseases of the liver or pancreas, hormonal and metabolic imbalances, and poisoning. Diarrhea must always be taken seriously if it is accompanied by other signs of illness, such as apathetic behavior, refusal to eat, or fever. Also important are the appearance and consistency of the feces: water, mushy, mixed with blood or mucus. If diarrhea in an adult cat lasts for more than 48 hours, it needs to go to the vet, since its body can no longer compensate for the continuing loss of fluid and nutrients. If the cat is otherwise perky and has no other signs of illness, often the following diet plan proves helpful: no food for 12 to no more than 24 hours, to relieve the strain on stomach and intestines, and then a period of 3 to 5 days with only easily digestible food. This can include low-fat farmer's cheese, cottage cheese, mashed potatoes (thinned with water), chicken with rice, or a specially formulated diet food (usually chicken or lamb with rice) that most veterinarians have on hand. Start with numerous, small meals spread throughout the day to help the irritated

INFO

Worming

Most young animals have worms; that's why kittens are first wormed at the early age of 2 weeks. Cats that go outside need worm treatments one to four times a year, since they can become infected by eating the rodents they catch. For indoor pets, however, one worming a year is normally sufficient. Alternatively, the vet can perform routine fecal checks. Worm your pet about 2 weeks before its annual booster shots are scheduled.

stomach readjust gradually to solid food. Make sure the cat gets plenty of fluids during the entire time; besides water, you can offer your pet weak black tea or chamomile tea. Young cats are physically far less robust. They lack the resistance to go without food altogether, and you should wait no more than 24 hours before taking them to the vet.

142. Drooling: What causes heavy drooling or slobbering?

Drooling is caused by a variety of feline diseases. For a correct diagnosis, therefore, other symptoms must be taken into account as well.

➤ Inflammations of the oral mucosa. Other symptoms: bad breath and refusal to eat.

➤ Foreign body in the throat. Other symptoms: choking and breathing difficulties.

➤ Poisonings. Frequently very heavy slobbering. Other symptoms often mixed: in some cases, trembling, diarrhea, spasms, paralysis, low temperature.

➤ Epilepsy. Typical symptoms: twitching, seizures, anxiety states, loss of consciousness.

➤ Rabies. Other symptoms: jumpiness, spasms, aggressiveness, paralysis.

➤ Slobbering. This is also a sign of uneasiness, for example, in cats that don't like riding in a car. Attendant symptoms: wailing, vomiting, and sweaty paws.

143. Drug intolerance: What symptoms will tell me whether a cat has an intolerance to its medication?

Most pet medications are only available by prescription and must be prescribed by a veterinarian after a thorough diagnosis. This requirement for a prescription limits the risks of endangering the cat's health and of possible side effects due to medicating your cat yourself in the absence of a prescription from the vet. Here especially, intolerance reactions frequently occur when medications are used by nonprofessionals. Typical symptoms are diarrhea, vomiting, mucus or foam coming from the mouth and nose, shortness of breath, swellings in the head region and the mucous membranes of the head, lurching gait. In all cases, the immediate attention of a veterinarian is required.

144. Ear mites: My male cat repeatedly scratches one ear. Do I need to take him to the vet?

Your tom quite probably has an inflammation of the external auditory canal, caused by ear mites (*Otodectes cynotis*). Although mange almost always affects both ears, usually one ear is more affected and causes more intense itching, which means that the cat scratches that ear more. Other symptoms include shaking its head and a dark-brown, crusty coating in the auditory canal. Afflicted animals must be kept separate, since ear mange can be communicated to other cats (as well as dogs). Especially at risk are young cats. The vet will make the exact diagnosis, since bacteria and fungi, in addition to mites, can cause ear infections. If a foreign body (grass awn) has gotten stuck in the ear, the cat will also scratch and shake its head in an attempt to dislodge it.

145. Epilepsy: Can epileptic seizures in cats be cured?

In an epileptic seizure there are powerful, uncontrolled electrical charges inside the brain. Depending on the cause, the course and symptoms of epilepsy can vary widely. With serious seizures, the cat can no longer control its movements; it twitches, falls to the ground, and loses consciousness. Typical attendant symptoms are salivation, hair standing on end, noises, release of urine and feces. More common in cats is mild epilepsy, with trembling, twitching of ears, whiskers, and individual muscle groups, impaired consciousness, and dilated pupils. Since no overall spasms appear, the owner often doesn't even notice the seizures. Not atypical, however, are other forms in which the cat runs around aimlessly, chases nonexistent objects, or threatens an imaginary enemy. The search for the causes of the epilepsy is not always easy. Besides organic disorders and changes in the brain of the type caused by circulatory problems, tumors, abscesses, or infections, metabolic diseases of the kidneys or liver not infrequently play a role, as do poisonings. The first time a cat has an epileptic seizure, you should take it to the vet immediately.

> ### EXTRA TIP
>
> **Taking temperature**
> This is easiest if a second person holds the cat by the chest and front legs. Hold your pet's tail to one side and insert the thermometer about ¾ inch (2 cm) into its anus. Whatever you do, don't let go of the thermometer! With a digital thermometer, you have a read-out in a few seconds. The normal temperature of an adult cat is between 100.4 and 102.7°F (38.0 and 39.3°C).

In addition to thorough monitoring of its state of health and blood tests, neurological examinations are often required. In most cases, the vet will recommend antiepileptic drug therapy, which must be administered for the rest of the cat's life. No cure for epilepsy is possible, but with the proper doses of drugs, the seriousness, length, and frequency of the seizures can be moderated. That is very important for the affected animal because the risk of brain damage increases with every seizure, especially if it is prolonged, or if several seizures occur within a short time.

146. Euthanasia: Our old tom obviously is in great pain and can scarcely move anymore. Should we release him from his misery?

If your tomcat is visibly suffering and there is no way to ease his pain, you should not prolong his agony. The vet will put him to sleep with an anesthetic so gently that he won't notice a thing. You need to be at his side in these last few minutes. Your closeness means a lot, and you can say goodbye to a friend who was part of your life for many years. If there are no legal obstacles, you can bury him in your own yard. For information, contact the regulatory agency or the local authorities. If you have no property of your own, you can bury your cat in a pet cemetery or take it to a pet crematorium.

147. Eyes: **What eye problems are most common in cats?**

Cats frequently suffer from conjunctivitis. If the inflammation affects only one eye, foreign bodies (such as grain awns) or drafty air are usually to blame. Especially susceptible are short-nosed breeds such as Persians, whose wide-set eyes are only partly protected by the lids. Conjunctivitis in both eyes is often a result of infections (such as rhinotracheitis). Symptoms of conjunctivitis: reddening and swelling of the conjunctiva, tearing or discharge from the eyes, prolapse of the nictitating membrane. The trip to the vet must not be put off, since persistent inflammation can damage the cornea and impair the cat's vision. Like conjunctivitis, keratitis (inflammation of the cornea) is triggered by foreign bodies or infections.

148. Eyes: **Is a cat sick if you can't see its nictitating membrane?**

The cat's nictitating membrane has the function of a third eyelid; it protects the eye from dust, dirt, and foreign bodies and ensures that the eye is always kept sufficiently moist. Normally the thin membrane is concealed in the corner of the eye, and in a healthy cat only a tiny portion of it at most moves across the eye when the animal is tired. A constantly visible nictitating membrane, however, is not always a sign that the cat is feeling poorly or weak, or is even seriously ill. Prolapse of the membrane is typical in conjunctivitis, infectious diseases, and worm infestation. Only the veterinarian can make an exact diagnosis.

149. Fleas: Can fleas transmit diseases to cats? ?

Flea bites cause intense itching. The cat scratches itself constantly, which leads to inflammation of the sites of the bites and may cause hair loss. A bad infestation not infrequently results in allergic eczema. Young animals are affected even more seriously than adult cats, and often they become anemic and emaciated. Fleas must be brought under control, not least of all because they are also intermediate hosts for tapeworms. In direct contact with other cats, it is usually cat fleas that are transmitted, but other types of fleas (such as dog fleas) may afflict cats as well. Flea control efforts must always include the places where the cat rests and sleeps, since only mature fleas are found on the host animal, where they suck blood, while flea eggs and larvae are concealed in cushions, pillows, sheets, and cracks in wood in the surrounding area. These developmental stages can be successfully eliminated only by repeatedly using a special flea-control agent and a vacuum cleaner against the parasites. Don't forget to spray the inside of the vacuum cleaner bag regularly with a flea spray as well. To get rid of

Cats that go outdoors are more susceptible to parasites than indoor cats. Checking your pet's coat on a regular basis offers the best protection.

A flea collar will ward off the troublesome pests. A break-away collar that opens under pressure will keep the cat from getting the collar caught on something.

FIRST AID

Quick and careful first aid can save a cat's life in an emergency and also improve the chances of success of any emergency procedures initiated later by the veterinarian. For these

BLEEDING WOUNDS
Clean the injured area, apply cellulose or paper tissues, and wrap with a cloth, sock, or necktie. The emergency dressing must be tight to stop the bleeding.

BROKEN BONES
If at all possible, lay the injured animal so that there is no strain on the site of the fracture. Don't try any further treatment on your own; just keep the cat warm and take it to the vet at once.

POISONINGS
Common symptoms of poisoning are drooling, vomiting, cramps, and collapse. Get the cat to a vet without delay. If possible, bring along the toxic substance (packaging, package insert) or poisonous plant.

BURNS
Dab the burned area with water, or apply a bag of ice. If the area is large, cover it with a cloth or bandaging material.

WASP STINGS
If possible, remove the stinger and cool the site of the sting with ice or cold water. For stings in the mouth and throat area, take the cat to the vet immediately (danger of suffocation).

BITES
Bites from dogs and other cats cause wounds that don't look serious but are quite deep, and they can result in ugly abscesses. If in doubt, take the cat to the vet immediately.

reasons, every cat owner should know the most important first-aid techniques and methods. In particular, cats that go outdoors are exposed to many dangers.

FOREIGN BODY IN THE THROAT
Hold the cat's head from the back and press on the corners of its mouth until it opens; then remove the foreign body with tweezers. If you can't get hold of the object, take your pet to the vet at once.

LOSS OF CONSCIOUSNESS
Stretch out the unconscious cat on its right side. Open its mouth, pull the tongue out slightly, and clear the respiratory passages (for example, of vomit). Keep the cat warm with a blanket.

SHOCK
Symptoms of shock are shallow breathing, pale mucous membranes, and cold paws. Often, the cat exhibits apathetic behavior. Lay the body on one side, ensure that the cat can breathe freely and has fresh air, and keep it from getting chilled.

PANIC
Symptoms of panic are irrational, sometimes even aggressive behavior. If possible, wrap the cat in a cloth to keep it from running away, injuring itself, or trying to bite.

INJURIES FROM A FALL
In addition to broken bones and jaws, internal injuries are relatively common. Even cats that appear unharmed should be examined by a vet, therefore.

TRANSPORTATION TO THE VET
Ideally, transport your cat in a pet carrier. If one is not available, carefully lay your pet on a blanket or on a stable surface if there is a spinal injury.

119

the fleas on the cat itself, there are various methods of treatment: spot-on preparations that are dripped on the back of the neck and offer protection lasting several weeks or months, in addition to tablets, homeopathic remedies, scented oils, and shampooing lotions. If the cat has an allergic reaction to certain active ingredients (such as those used in flea collars), you need to decide on a suitable treatment in consultation with the veterinarian.

150. Fox tapeworm: How high is the risk that a human will become infected with the fox tapeworm by a cat?

In Germany, the fox tapeworm, *Echinococcus multiocularis,* is especially widespread in the southern part of the country and in eastern Germany. Its principal host is the red fox, and 70% of the red fox population is infected with the parasite. Afflicted animals pass the tapeworm eggs in their stool. The further development of the tapeworm takes place in rodents that eat these eggs. Humans become involved by coming into contact with cats that have eaten infected mice and excrete worm eggs. Since foxes appear with increasing frequency in the outskirts of urban areas and sometimes even in the city center itself, there is a risk of infections in parks and urban green areas too, besides the risk previously existing only for cats (and dogs) in rural areas. If your cat goes outdoors, you should have

INFO

Toxoplasmosis
Toxoplasmosis is an infectious disease caused by single-celled parasites. Cats that go outdoors are at higher risk than indoor cats, since they can contract the disease from prey. Humans, too, can get the disease by coming in contact with infectious cat feces or eating infected raw pork. A toxoplasmosis test will show whether antibodies have formed in a person's blood to protect him or her against disease (important in the case of pregnant women).

your vet check its feces at regular intervals even if the probability of infestation is slight. If the check does reveal the presence of the fox tapeworm's eggs, they can be combated with a specific anthelminthic (dewormer). Humans can also be directly infected with the fox tapeworm by ingesting mushrooms, wild berries, or other fruits contaminated with fox feces without thoroughly washing them first.

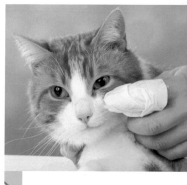

Tearstains and crusty patches beneath the eyes are best removed with a dampened tissue.

151. Grooming: How can I remove my Persian's unsightly tearstains?

In short-nosed breeds such as Persians, the nasolacrimal duct is very narrow. Tearing eyes and tearstains are not unusual in these cats. Dab the eyes regularly with a cotton pad dampened with hot water. The crusty patches usually can be removed this way as well. To prevent coat discoloration, use Vaseline, applied beneath the tearing eye. If the tear duct is totally blocked (usually due to an inflammation), the eyes will tear constantly. The vet will attempt to reopen the duct by flushing it. Discharge from an eye is a typical symptom of conjunctivitis.

152. Hair: Does a cat shed all year long?

Except for a few breeds (such as Rex cats), cats lose hair all the time. This applies particularly to indoor

THE RIGHT GROOMING TOOLS

Part of a thorough, gentle grooming of a cat's body and coat is using the right tools. They protect the cat against injury and pain and make the grooming process easier. Cats that are

ABSORBENT COTTON
It is easiest to clean eyes (including tearstains), ear flaps, paws, and claws with a dampened piece of absorbent cotton (alternative: soft, lint-free cloth).

NATURAL-BRISTLE BRUSH

Soft natural bristles brush out the coat and massage it to make the coat shiny. Combination brushes with natural bristles and wire bristles may also be used.

CHAMOIS
The coat acquires a long-lasting sheen when it is rubbed with chamois. Allergic reactions (see Info, page 33) can be lessened if the coat is regularly rubbed down with the dampened chamois.

RUBBER CURRY BRUSH
Rubber curry pads or gloves can also be used to remove dead hair from the coats of short-haired cats and to stimulate circulation.

SCISSORS AND TWEEZERS
The scissors are used to cut bandaging material to size and to trim hair. The tweezers are for removing foreign bodies. Use only those models with rounded tips.

COMBS
The small-tooth comb with close-set teeth removes dirt and foreign bodies. Wide-tooth combs remove dead hair.

accustomed in early youth to grooming procedures enjoy the gentle treatment as much as an hour of cuddling and petting.

CLAW CLIPPERS

Use claw clippers for trimming claws (see Tip, page 138). Don't use normal scissors; there's a high risk of cutting into the quick.

PET SHAMPOO

To bathe a cat, use only a gentle, moisturizing shampoo labeled as safe for use on cats. Shampoos for human use strip natural oils from the cat's skin.

MALT PASTE

Promotes and regulates digestion. Alternative: olive oil and anti-hairball snack (commercially available). Does not replace the bowl of cat grass.

FLEA POWDER AND SPOT-ON PREPARATIONS

Use flea powder and flea shampoo to combat fleas and flea collars and spot-on preparations (trickled onto the neck, it spreads over the skin) to prevent fleas. Use only products labeled as safe for cats.

TOOTHBRUSH AND PET TOOTHPASTE

Use a pet toothbrush or child's toothbrush and toothpaste formulated for pets (various flavors available in specialty stores).

VACUUM CLEANER

The vacuum cleaner (special attachments available) keeps the cat's sleeping place free of fleas and other parasites. Spray out the vacuum cleaner bag regularly with flea spray.

cats, which live in an environment with artificial light and a constant temperature. Animals that go outdoors shed less, especially if they are allowed to go out during the cold season. During molting in spring and fall, hair loss increases, and not infrequently hair falls out in bunches. Shedding cycles in spring and fall are triggered by the lengthening and shortening of daylight hours. At this time, longhaired cats need even more grooming than usual because they are unable to cope with the quantity of dead hair on their own. Shorthaired cats should be brushed more often when molting, with a natural-bristle brush and a rubber pad. The massage stimulates the circulation in the skin, which ultimately decreases hair loss. Rugs and sofas will remain largely free of cat hair if you frequently run dampened hands or a chamois over your pet's coat, thus removing a majority of the loose hair directly. Special attachments for the vacuum cleaner make it easier to keep your home clean. Unlike normal shedding, disease-related hair loss results in extreme thinning of the coat. Alternatively, hair loss may be restricted to certain areas of the body, as when the cat suffers from a mania for washing and licks its abdomen or thighs continually.

153. Handicap: After an accident, one of my cat's front legs was amputated. Can my pet still have a life worth living?

Even if a cat can only hop along on three legs, it still copes amazingly well with the loss. Inevitably, moving around is more tiring for your pet than for other cats, and its rest breaks may be a bit longer, but overall the handicap scarcely impairs its urge to be active. Even jumping is doable, and there are even cats that manage, with their remaining front leg, to press down on a door handle in mid-leap and open a door. Since the spine and joints are subjected to relatively great stress by the unusual mode of locomotion, the cat should be checked regularly by the vet. Cats that have lost a front leg need special assistance with grooming.

154. Handling: How do I hold my cat to keep it from hurting itself or others when it is undergoing treatment?

Cats are not always cooperative when they are being treated. These handling techniques will protect the cat and the persons doing the treating from injury:
➤ Nape hold: Grasp the coat at the back of the neck with your right hand, and put your left hand on the cat's back. Push down on the cat with both hands.
➤ Chest hold: With both thumbs at the back of the cat's neck, place your other fingers around its chest, in front of and behind its front legs.
➤ Wrapping: Cats that resist violently have to be wrapped in a blanket. Leave the animal's head free.

155. Harvest mites: Should I keep my cat indoors in fall to protect it against mites?

If your cat is allowed outside, it is unlikely to accept a ban on going out. You can combat the mites with sprays that are also used to control fleas. Check the cat in late summer and fall every time it comes back indoors. The parasites, which resemble tiny, yellowish dots, appear mainly on the head and abdomen and between the toes. These are the larvae; adult harvest mites live in the ground. Affected sites quickly become inflamed because the cat will scratch constantly. The vet will treat the sites locally with a suit-

INFO

Common symptoms of disease in older cats
➤ Loss of appetite: with kidney and liver diseases
➤ Emaciation: with chronic gastroenteritis
➤ Bad breath: with dental plaque and kidney disease
➤ Incontinence: with cystitis, bladder stones, and renal gravel
➤ Reluctance to move around: with arthrosis
➤ Intense thirst: with diabetes, kidney and liver problems
➤ Frequent urination: with diabetes and kidney infection

able active agent, and if large areas are affected, an insecticide bath will be prescribed. Harvest mites can afflict humans as well, but the cat is not a carrier.

A cotton square keeps the ear flap (pinna) clean. Cleaning the auditory canal, however, is a matter for the veterinarian alone.

156. Health check: How often should I check to see whether my cat is fit and healthy?

Check your pet every day! The health inspection takes almost no time and will give you an easy conscience. Here's how to do a 3-minute check:

➤ Behavior: normal, alert, curious, and sociable, and in no way aggressive.
➤ Mobility: no discernible problems moving around, jumping, and climbing.
➤ Coat: sleek and thick, not soiled, with no bald spots and matted areas, free of parasites.
➤ Skin: freed of crusted areas, wounds, inflammations, and knots (run your hands over the cat's body).
➤ Body: abdomen and flanks neither sunken nor swollen.
➤ Eyes: clear and free of discharge; conjunctiva is pale pink, nictitating membrane not visible.
➤ Ears: clean, odor-free, and with no coatings.
➤ Nose: dry, warm, and with no discharge.
➤ Mouth and teeth: teeth free of plaque. Gums and mucosa pink in color. The cat does not have bad breath.
➤ Paws and claws: pads have no wounds or cracks, no foreign bodies between the pads. The claws are not too long and are neither torn nor split.
➤ Anus: clean, hairs not stuck together.
➤ Excretions: no problems using the toilet. The stool is well formed, the urine free of blood and discoloration.

➤ Breathing: even, quickly returns to normal after physical activity.

➤ Appetite: The cat has a good appetite and eats the normal amount of food; it does not drink noticeably more or less than usual. If possible, take away any mice that your pet brings home, and give it a little treat as a substitute.

157. Health insurance: **What is covered by a health insurance policy for cats?**

Several insurance carriers also offer health insurance for cats. Generally the policy covers veterinary care with vaccinations, worming, and check-ups, as well as out-patient and in-patient care and medications. Coverage does not include diet food, grooming accessories, certificates, tattooing, and castration. Healthy animals between the ages of 2 months and 9 years are eligible to receive coverage. The amount of the contribution depends on the age of the cat and its lifestyle (indoor or indoor-outdoor cat), and it is higher for purebred cats than for mixed breeds. There are special policies that cover the costs of surgery for your pet.

158. Heart disease: **What can cause hypertrophic cardiomyopathy?**

In feline hypertrophic cardiomyopathy (HCM or HKM), individual heart muscles thicken and the left chamber of the heart is enlarged. Depending on the severity of the disease, the weakening of the heart can also lead to heart failure. Research on the causes of feline HCM is still in its infancy. For some breeds (Maine Coon, American Shorthair), the disease has been shown to be inherited. Possibly other diseases such as hyperthyroidism and hypertension also play a role. HCM can appear in cats of any age. For diagnosis, sound imaging (echocardiogram) is required. Lack of taurine in the diet has also been associated with heart problems.

159. Hygiene: In dealing with my cat, where do I have to pay special attention to cleanliness?

Effective hygiene includes clean living conditions and conscientious health care for your pet. Proper everyday hygiene has various components: regular cleaning (if needed, disinfection as well) of places where the cat rests and sleeps, baskets, blankets, and toys, in addition to daily washing of the food and water bowls and cleaning of the litter box. Health care procedures include full protection provided by vaccination with annual booster shots, worming, careful grooming of body and coat with suitable steps to protect against parasites, species-appropriate housing, balanced diet, and regular checkups by a veterinarian. Keeping your cat healthy also lowers the risk of transmitting a disease to humans (see Zoonoses, pages 153).

160. In heat: Is spaying the only way to keep a cat from going into heat?

The cat's heat (estrus) cycles can be suppressed by a hormone preparation, which must be administered once a week. Since cats frequently spit out or throw up tablets, this method is not totally reliable. As an alternative, there is a contraceptive injection that can be given after heat and then at 4-month intervals. The heat cycles can be regulated with progesterone tablets. Long-term treatment with hormones increases susceptibility to inflammations of the uterus and especially raises the risk of mammary gland tumors. To rule out health problems, spaying is the method of choice to prevent offspring for any cat that is not slated to be used for breeding.

161. Incontinence: My 14-year-old cat is dribbling urine. Is this normal in elderly felines?

When the release of urine can't be controlled, kidney disease or inflammations of the urinary tract and bladder are usually responsible. These diseases are more common in older animals (see Info, page 125). Since they can seriously damage the entire organism, you should take your pet to the vet immediately.

162. Incubation period: How long can it take for the first symptoms of disease to appear after an infection?

Incubation period is the term used for the time from a germ's entry into the body until the appearance of the first symptoms of disease. Depending on the disease, the incubation period can be several hours, but often several months or even years. For cat flu it is 2–5 days; for rabies, 14–30 days; for infectious peritonitis (FIP), up to 4 months. With leukemia (FeLV) and Feline Immunodeficiency Virus ("cat AIDS," FIV), several years may pass before signs of disease appear.

163. Infectious diseases: Which germs are especially dangerous for cats?

Infectious diseases are a serious threat to a cat's health. Most are viral in origin, and a few are caused

Happy companionship: Seniors, both human and feline, value peace and quiet, closeness, and a feeling of security.

Dreaming in a cozy bed: Senior cats need more sleep and longer recovery times than their younger kin.

by bacteria. Only preventive inoculations can give a cat effective protection against most life-threatening infections (see Vaccination Schedule, page 106).

➤ Cat flu (feline rhinotracheitis): contagious infectious disease, primarily transmitted from one cat to another by coughing and sneezing. Symptoms: fever, ulcers, discharge of pus from eyes and nose. Young cats are especially at risk.

➤ Feline distemper (FP, panleukopenia): Transmitted in direct contact and via objects. Symptoms: poor appetite, vomiting, watery to bloody diarrhea, inactivity. It is highly contagious, and the pathogen is extremely resistant.

➤ Calici virus: Serious upper respiratory infection. Symptoms: sneezing, nasal discharge, poor appetite, painful tongue, mouth ulcers, sore muscles. Vaccine is preventive.

➤ Feline leukemia (FeLV, Feline Leukemia Virus): Transmitted through saliva and excretions. Sometimes an incubation period of several years with no signs of disease. Symptoms (quite variable): weakness, loss of appetite, fever, emaciation, abscesses, tumors of internal organs.

➤ Feline Infectious Peritonitis (FIP): Many infected animals may be symptom-free. Stress promotes the outbreak of the diseases, which may be transmitted by direct contact. Symptoms: fever, poor appetite, emaciation, in some cases accumulation of fluid in the abdomen or inflammation of kidneys, liver, and spleen.

➤ Feline Immunodeficiency Virus (FIV, "cat AIDS"): Usually transmitted through bites. Symptoms (often only years later): fever, weakness, anemia, tumors, secondary infections. Though related to HIV, it cannot be transmitted to humans. A vaccine is available.

➤ Rabies: Transmitted in the saliva of infected foxes and other wild animals. Symptoms: restlessness, jumpiness, spasms, drooling, aggressiveness, paralysis. Unvaccinated animals must be euthanized if rabies is suspected. Rabies must be reported to the authorities, and vaccination is required by law in many localities. Humans too can become infected.

➤ Toxoplasmosis: Transmitted by raw meat, prey, and the feces of infected young cats. Adult cats usually are symptom-free, but unborn kittens can be harmed. Toxoplasmosis is communicable to humans, but generally does not cause symptoms (see Info, page 120). Those endangered are people with weakened immune systems and pregnant women, in whom an infection can cause miscarriage or damage the fetus.

164. Licking problem: **Is it pathological if a cat licks itself constantly?**

Cats are very clean and wash themselves thoroughly several times a day. Coat grooming is pathological if the cat is harming itself in the process and keeps licking the same places over and over mainly on the abdomen and the insides of the legs. The compulsion to wash leads to hair loss and skin inflammations. This behavior often is triggered by stress (for example, if the cat is oppressed by dominant members of its species or is being improperly cared for) or by boredom (usually with indoor cats). Hormone doses can provide relief, but relapses are not infrequent. Often, however, a behavioral disorder is also a symptom of physical problems. The cause of the grooming mania might be a skin disease, for example.

165. Limping: **If my cat is limping, should I take it to the vet right away?**

First check the paws: Sometimes the cause is only hairs that are stuck together, little stones, and in summer pieces of softened tar that get in between the pads and are relatively easy to remove. Cracks,

A healthy cat runs, jumps, and climbs without visible hindrance. Every mobility problem is an alarm signal.

wounds, and firmly embedded foreign bodies must be treated by the vet. If there is a strain, sprain, or bruise, the injured or inflamed joint will be swollen and be warm to the touch. Usually the cat won't put any pressure on the limb at all. This is also true with inflammations of the cellular tissue (phlegmon), when germs have gotten under the skin through a wound, which can happen with relative ease after a cat has been bitten. A broken bone (after an accident or a fall) can usually be spotted because the leg is in an odd position. Important here is gentle handling when taking the cat to the vet.

166. Mange: How do you protect a cat against mange? **?**

Mange is caused by grass mites (*Sarcoptes*). The vet will make the diagnosis after microscopic examination of a skin scraping and prescribe a special mange remedy. As long as the infestation is localized, the treatment will quickly yield results. For this reason, cats that go outdoors should be examined regularly for mites in order to initiate therapy immediately, if required. Because of the high risk of contagion, afflicted animals must be kept separate. Mange is also communicable to humans.

167. Massage: Do massages have the same beneficial effect on a cat as on us humans? **?**

Most cats find massages just as pleasant as being petted. In contrast to petting, in massage the hands must exert a gentle, well-calculated pressure in order to stimulate circulation in the skin. That also will work with a soft brush of the sort used for daily grooming. With a little practice, you can quickly tell which massage strokes get a really positive reaction from your cat. Therapeutic massage, however, should be left to a professional or attempted only after detailed guidance. It is used specifically after diseases of the musculoskeletal system and for follow-up treatment of muscle injuries. So-called effleurage, with gentle rhythmic stroking in a certain direction, serves primarily to relax, while the petrissage that follows is intended to promote circulation in individual skin and muscle areas by kneading, rolling, and squeezing.

168. Mastitis: What causes inflammation of the mammary glands, and what happens to the kittens then?

An inflammation of the mammary glands (mastitis) is usually the result of milk blockage. It occurs when the queen has too few kittens and they drink only part of her milk, but it can also occur when she is still lactating but no longer nursing her young. Inflammation results when bacteria form in the remaining milk. The inflamed tissue swells, hardens, and causes the cat visible pain. She usually is apathetic, has fever, refuses food and water, and frequently even rejects the kittens. To halt the inflammation, the vet will prescribe antibiotics and anti-inflammatories. The owner can promote healing by applying cooling compresses to the mammary glands.

The kittens should be separated from their mother and hand-reared or nursed by a foster mother. Since the kittens would come into contact with germs through their mother's milk, this applies even if the mother cat has not rejected them. If a queen has too few kittens to nurse, milk blockage and the risk of

INFO

Cats help heal

Cats lend encouragement and promote self-confidence; even their mere presence has a corrective, soothing effect. This is true especially for older people, as well as for those with physical and mental ailments. In homes for the aged and nursing facilities, cats are used with increasing frequency as visitor animals. Therapists and psychologists include them in pet-supported therapies, and hospitals and rehab centers also are discovering that the cat has an aura that promotes healing.

mastitis can be prevented by putting additional, usually orphaned, kittens in the birthing box.

169. Medicating your cat yourself: Is it all right for me to give my cat medications on my own?

Quite a number of people dispense with the trip to the doctor when they are feeling unwell or even have unmistakable symptoms of disease; instead, they supply themselves with medicine from the drugstore or rely on household remedies, a questionable and frequently high-risk form of self-medication. If you try this with your cat, you are putting your pet's life at risk.
➤ Even experienced owners often misinterpret their pet's symptoms. Supposedly slight illnesses then drag on because the medicine is not strong enough, while harmless maladies are treated with overly powerful remedies.
➤ Preparations used in human medicine can cause intolerance reactions and poisoning.
➤ If you use guidelines based on human medicine in determining the dosage, you are endangering your pet's life, since the patient's body weight and specific metabolic rate must be taken into account with every medication. Even a pharmacist can't give a pet owner information here. Most medications used in animal medicine require a prescription for good reason: They can be properly used only after the vet has made a diagnosis.

170. Medicine: Can I treat my cat with medicines from our household medicine cabinet?

No, the cat's body reacts to many substances in a completely different way from a human's body. Giving a cat medications from our medicine cabinet can lead to gastric bleeding, spasms, changes in blood count, liver and kidney damage, and many other problems and illnesses. For example, acetaminophen is highly toxic to cats, and even two tablets with the active agent acetylsalicylic acid (aspirin) are fatal for cats. Therefore, treating a cat with preparations used in human medicine is absolutely taboo. To avoid mix-ups, you should always store the cat's medications in a separate place. Ideally, reserve a special little cupboard for the feline medicine chest (see overview, page 136).

171. Medicine: How do you give a cat tablets and drops?

➤ Eye drops and ointments: Hold the eyelids slightly open and trickle the drops under the upper lid; apply the ointment in a thin strand. Always apply eye medicine from one side, never from directly in front.

➤ Ear drops: Lift up the ear flap, slowly trickle in the drops, and then massage the base of the ear.

➤ Tablets: Test to see which delivery method works best with your pet. Method 1: Hold the cat's head from the back, and press the corners of its mouth, using your thumb and index finger, until your pet's mouth opens. Place the tablet on the tongue as far back as possible, close its mouth, and keep it closed until the cat has swallowed the medicine. Method 2: Dissolve the tablet in water and trickle it into the cat's mouth from one side, using a disposable syringe (minus the needle). Method 3: Crush the tablet and mix it in the cat's food. Method 4: Pulverize the tablet, mix it with vitamin paste or farmer cheese, and spread it on a front paw. Ask your vet in advance whether the medication can be added to something without losing any of its effectiveness.

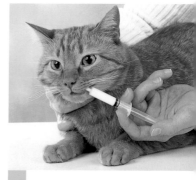

Liquid nutrients and medicine in liquid form are administered by trickling them into one side of the cat's mouth with a disposable syringe (minus the needle).

MEDICINE CHEST FOR YOUR CAT

A cat's medicine chest should contain everything needed to keep your pet healthy, care for it when it is ill, and treat minor injuries and complaints.

BANDAGING MATERIAL

Cotton padding, bandage gauze, band-aids, adhesive tape, elastic bandages in various widths (2 and 4 inches (5 and 10 cm)), and sterile compresses are essential elements.

DISPOSABLE GLOVES

Protect humans against germs and lower the risk of contamination or infection when dealing with open wounds and fractures.

DISPOSABLE SYRINGES

Disposable syringes (minus the needle) in various sizes are needed when squirting drops or liquid nourishment into the cat's mouth.

DISINFECTANT SPRAY

Alcohol-free sprays are suitable for disinfecting wounds. The agent must be free of phenols and iodine-containing substances. Ask your vet for a recommendation.

TWEEZERS AND SCISSORS

Tweezers will remove foreign bodies, and scissors can be used to trim the hair around the edges of a wound. Make sure both implements have rounded tips.

FLEA-CONTROL PRODUCTS

Spot-on preparations are dripped onto the back of a cat's neck and afford protection against fleas for several weeks. Some cats have a sensitive reaction to the active agents in flea collars.

It also is used for first aid in an emergency, before the veterinarian arrives. If the symptoms are serious or unclear, however, the cat should always be seen first by a veterinarian.

TICK REMOVAL DEVICE
A tick removal device gets rid of the parasites with a little twist and ensures that the tick's head does not remain in the skin.

WORM CONTROL AGENT
For use in periodic control of worms, chiefly in cats that go outdoors (see Info, page 112), in suspected cases of worm infestation, and in the event of possible tapeworm infestation after treatment for fleas.

OINTMENT FOR WOUNDS
For use in caring for scratches and minor wounds. Vaseline keeps the pads of the paws from developing cracks in winter (but cats sometimes lick it off).

CLINICAL THERMOMETER
Cats rarely will hold still to have their temperature taken. Well suited for this purpose is a digital thermometer (see Tip, page 115), which displays the temperature reading quickly.

ADDITIONAL SUPPLIES
A wool blanket keeps a sick or injured animal from getting chilled and also is useful for transporting it; plastic bags can be used to cover a bandaged paw.

ONLY IF NEEDED
Eye drops and eye ointments, eardrops, and medicinal baths should be bought only if directed by the veterinarian and should not be stockpiled. Note the expiration date.

172. Obligation to report: Which feline diseases must be reported to the authorities? ?

There is a reporting requirement for certain infectious diseases that are communicable to humans (see Zoonoses, page 153). The reporting requirement applies to rabies, salmonellosis, and infectious diseases caused by parasites, such as giardiosis, echinococcosis (fox and dog tapeworm), and, under certain circumstances, also toxoplasmosis.

173. Pet cemetery: One day I want to bury my cat in a pet cemetery. What do I need to keep in mind? ?

Under certain covenants, you are permitted to bury your pet in your own yard or garden. If that is not possible, the pet cemetery is the right choice. The costs of interment depend on the size of the animal and may differ from one cemetery to another. The pet cemetery may have certain requirements about what type of coffin can be used for burial. The styling of the gravesite is generally left to the pet owner. The gravesite can be reserved in advance. In addition to burial, many cemeteries also offer cremation. Since many pet owners want to pay frequent visits to the grave of their beloved cat, you should choose a cemetery near where you live and make sure it is easily reachable by public transportation.

EXTRA TIP

Clipping claws
Cats neglect the care of their claws only in exceptional cases (for example, when ill or extremely old). Overly long claws can be trimmed with a special nail clipper. To avoid injuring the pink tissue (the quick), cut off only the very tip of the claw. Your vet will be glad to demonstrate the proper technique for you. Normally hidden, the claw will emerge if you gently press your thumb and index finger on the pad of the paw.

174. Placenta: Should I let the mother cat eat the placentas?

The placenta mediates metabolic exchange between mother and fetus. It is expelled at birth or shortly thereafter. Since the placenta also contains many valuable nutrients, it is a good source of energy for the queen, weakened by giving birth. Further, it simultaneously stimulates her milk production. You need not be concerned if your cat eats the placentas.

175. Poisoning: What are the typical symptoms of poisoning?

Cats relatively seldom are poisoned because, with the exception of kittens, they are unlikely to eat unfamiliar substances. Poisoning usually occurs when they nibble on poisonous house plants (see Info, page 46), or when their coat gets a poisonous substance on it and the cat licks itself clean. Signs of poisoning: slobbering and vomiting (caused, for example, by cleaning agents, disinfectants, and solvents); uncoordinated movements, spasms, and twitching (antifreeze); dilated pupils, bloody diarrhea, white mucosa (rat poison). Contact with gasoline and fuel oil leads to spasms and circulatory weakness, while turpentine causes nausea and liver damage. In every instance, notify the vet at once and, if at all possible, take the packaging or a sample of the toxin with you.

176. Pregnancy: Does a pregnant queen need special care and attention?

In the days before giving birth, the cat roams around the house and looks for a suitable birthing place, searching through armoires, chests, and drawers. Now is the time to offer her a wooden crate or sturdy carton for her "confinement" in a quiet, draft-free, darkened corner. That way you avoid the risk that she will deliver her young somewhere else; cats that go outdoors often have their young in concealed places that

Even indoor cats sometimes get outdoors and therefore should be vaccinated against rabies.

require a lot of searching to find. The birthing box should have a floor area of about 20 × 28 inches (50 × 70 cm) and a height of 8–12 inches (20–30 cm). Lay a thick, washable pillow in the box to keep away cold rising from the floor. Over it, place a blanket, several layers of newspaper, and clean cloths. Mothers-to-be are often peculiar when it comes to the choice of location. Put the box in a different place if she doesn't like your first choice. In the final days before her due date, don't let her go outdoors.

177. Pregnancy: When can you tell whether a cat is pregnant?

On about the fourteenth day after mating, the fertilized eggs become implanted in the uterus. From the twenty-fourth to twenty-eighth day, an ultrasound exam can be performed. Since the cat's uterus is Y-shaped, not all the young can be seen in this way. From the fortieth day on, X-ray examination is also possible. With ultrasound, the vet sees whether kittens are developing normally and whether any problems are likely during delivery.

The external signs of pregnancy can differ widely from cat to cat. In some expectant felines, they are so unobtrusive that the owner notices only in the last few days that kittens are on the way. In the first 3 weeks after mating, there are neither physical nor behavioral changes. Only then do the teats turn pink and become firmer. From the fifth week of pregnancy, the queen's abdomen becomes more or less evident and she gains depending on the number of young about 10 ounces (300 g) per week. She becomes increasingly domestic, calmer, and more affectionate, washes extensively and devotedly, develops an especially good appetite, and nibbles on cat grass more frequently.

178. Pseudopregnancy: What causes pseudopregnancy in a cat?

Ovulation in cats, unlike many other mammals, occurs in response to mating. In queens that are in heat, however, it can be induced by manual stimulation alone. In this case too, all the hormonal changes typical of pregnant females take place: The abdomen becomes more rounded, and often lactation also occurs. The apparently pregnant cat treats certain objects, such as her toys, like newborn kittens; she cleans and defends them. The pseudopregnancy can last up to 6 weeks. Repeated false pregnancy leads to inflammations of the mammary glands and uterus. Cats that have recurring pseudopregnancies must be spayed. After neutering, these problems will not reappear.

179. Rabies. As an exclusively indoor cat, my Somali never goes outside. Do I still have to have her vaccinated against rabies?

Even with attentive owners, cats can still manage to run away now and then. Even less adventurous breeds like Persians or Ragdolls may allow themselves a little neighborhood outing. That can be dangerous if you live at the edge of town or near woods, where your cat can come into contact with foxes that are infected with rabies. The disease is transmitted through bites, and an infected cat poses a considerable risk to humans as well. Animals that have not been vaccinated must be killed immediately upon suspicion of infection. Basically, to play it safe, have your cat vaccinated against rabies on an annual basis. Since foxes are increasingly common in the suburbs and even in urban inner cities, there is an increased risk here as well.

180. Ringworm: **What are the symptoms of a ringworm infestation, and how great is the risk of contagion for humans?**

Typical of a ringworm infestation are round bare patches with a reddish, inflamed margin, usually in the head area, but also on the legs, tail, and back. Because of the intense itching, the cat scratches itself almost uninterruptedly. Ringworm is not rare in cats. More than 90% of the cases are caused by the fungus, *Microsporum canis,* with which even animals that appear outwardly healthy (especially young cats) can be infected. *Microsporum canis* is one of the transmissible dermatophytes. Humans become infected primarily through direct contact, and children who cuddle and play with an infected cat are especially at risk. The microspore appears in the form of red spots, principally on the face, neck, hands, and forearms. The exact diagnosis must be made by a dermatologist. When dealing with an infected cat, be sure to observe strict hygiene procedures. Sick and healthy animals must be kept separate.

181. Roundworms: **Why are young cats so susceptible to worm infestations?**

In private homes, cats infected with roundworms pass the parasites' eggs, invisible to the naked eye, in their stools, and occasionally they also excrete the 2.5- to 4-inch (6- to 10-cm)-long mature worms. Other cats can acquire worms through the feces. Prey animals such as mice and birds are also a source of infection because the worms survive in them in a dormant stage. Roundworms go through several larval stages. Some of these worm larvae become encapsulated in the cat's musculature and often remain inactive there for a long period, with no visible signs of the infestation. If the cat later is in heat or pregnant, these larvae travel into the mammary glands and later are passed to the young in their mother's milk. Therefore, more than 90% of newborn kittens are infested with roundworms. The parasites are brought under control by repeated worming of the young and the nursing queen. Through worm eggs, humans can also become infected with the feline roundworm, *Toxocara mystax*. In an adult, the infection generally is harmless, but in children it often produces fever, coughing, stomachache, and eye problems such as strabismus and retinal changes.

182. Salmonellosis: How do cats get infected with salmonellosis?

Salmonella infections cause gastrointestinal inflammation in cats, and the animals are greatly weakened by vomiting and diarrhea. Possible sources of infection are spoiled food, uncooked offal and meat by-products, and raw poultry in particular. For these reasons, chicken and other poultry should be served only in roasted or boiled form. A great many of the infected cats exhibit no symptoms of any kind, but often they excrete the pathogens for years and can transmit the disease to other animals and to humans. In humans, a salmonella infection often takes the form of diarrhea. Conscientious hygiene especially in the case of children who have close contact with a cat reduces the risk of contagion.

183. Sterilization: What is the difference between sterilization and neutering?

Sterilization renders the female cat infertile and the male impotent. In the operation, the fallopian tubes or the spermatic cords are severed. Unlike neutering (see Info, page 148), sterilization does not eliminate the sex drive. Along with it, all the attendant phenomena such as roaming and spraying urine are retained. A sterilized female is continually in heat and has a tendency for cyst formation. In the U.S., sterilization is not commonly performed in cats.

SYMPTOMS OF DISEASE

SYMPTOMS	POSSIBLE CAUSES
Aggressiveness	Injuries, rabies
Apathy, fever, crawling off to hide	General symptoms of illness
Bad breath	Dental plaque, inflammation of oral mucosa, kidney inflammation
Constant scratching	Fleas, mites
Constipation	Inactivity, improper diet, hairballs
Coughing	Cold, allergies, infections
Diarrhea	Diseases of the stomach, intestines, liver, and pancreas, infections
Discharge from eyes	Blocked tear ducts, glaucoma, eye injuries
Drooling	Foreign body in throat, poisoning, inflammation of oral mucosa
Excessive appetite	Diabetes
Excessive thirst	Diabetes, kidney and liver diseases
Limping	Paw injuries, muscular strain, fracture
Loss of appetite	Worms, infections, hairballs, gastro-intestinal inflammations
Pathological loss of hair	Parasites, ringworm, psychological and hormonal disturbances
Prolapse of nictitating membrane	Conjunctivitis, worms, infections
Refusal to eat	Tartar, hairballs, infections, stress, foreign body in throat
"Sledding"	Blockage of anal sacs
Uncleanness	Gastrointestinal problems, obesity, psychological causes (such as stress)
Vomiting	Gastritis, stomach ulcers, infections, and many other causes
Weight loss	Worms, diabetes, fleas, infections

184. Tapeworms: How does a cat get infected with a tapeworm?

Cats can get infected with both the "cat" and the "dog" tapeworm primarily by eating mice and rats, frequently without the infestation causing any discernible symptoms. Diarrhea, loss of appetite, and severe weight loss usually occur only in young cats. In even rarer instances, cats can also acquire from their prey the dangerous fox tapeworm, which is a threat to human hosts as well. Cats that go outdoors should be wormed several times a year (see Info, page 112). For indoor cats, at least one worm treatment each year is helpful, as they too can contract tapeworms by eating fleas containing the larvae of the "cucumber tapeworm." Therefore, owners always must combat even a mild flea infestation.

185. Tartar: Our cat has a lot of tartar. Can this be brought under control?

Dental plaque and calculus (tartar) are the most common causes of dental problems and gum inflammations in cats. The formation of hard, brownish tooth deposits is promoted by a one-sided diet or a diet of soft food exclusively; it may also be attributable to a

1 *Regular visual inspection of the teeth will reveal deposits and pathological changes in the teeth at an early stage.*

2 *Not all cats are willing to swallow tablets. Sometimes you have to outsmart them with a little trick.*

hereditary predisposition (in Persians and others). Young cats, too, can be affected, but usually senior cats are troubled by these problems. If a cat has a tendency to form tartar, it can't be kept from forming altogether, but the process can be slowed by preventive measures. These include serving larger chunks of meat in the food bowl, which the cat has to break into smaller pieces. They will perform a mechanical cleaning of the teeth (especially the molars) and keep food remnants from getting stuck and leading to plaque formation and to tartar. Special snacks that clean teeth (found in specialty stores) have a similar effect. Despite its firm consistency, dry food does not really achieve the same purpose, since the little bits are broken up with a single bite or swallowed whole. Part of good dental hygiene for your cat is also regular brushing of the teeth. That works best if you get the cat accustomed to the procedure when it is still a kitten. Suitable for use are toothbrushes for children and special pet toothpaste (available in various flavors), which can be swallowed without concern, or a dampened cloth with precipitated chalk. If tartar has already formed, only the veterinarian can remove it. If the tartar buildup is heavy, the deposits must be removed with ultrasound while the cat is anesthetized.

> ### EXTRA TIP
>
> **Controlling odors**
> A healthy cat has almost no odor that can be picked up by the human nose. Bad breath, therefore, is always an alarm signal. An unpleasant ear odor is an indication of mites, and there is a sweetish smell if the cat's paws are sweating from fear or excitement. The saliva a cat spreads in its coat when washing has a subtle and slightly tart smell.

186. **Teething: How can you make the teething process easier for a kitten?**

The cat's milk teeth are replaced by the permanent teeth. Teething is completed between the fourth and seventh months of life, and the process begins later in a male kitten than in a female. In this troublesome phase, also give your pet larger pieces of food that require some chewing, in addition to the usual soft food. That strengthens the muscles used for chewing and speeds the teething process. Chew toys are also good for this purpose.

187. Ticks: Can ticks transmit diseases to cats?

In cats, tick bites usually lead only to local inflammations, but a heavier infestation sometimes causes itching. Whether cats can contract Lyme disease (borreliosis) from infected ticks is not yet certain (for dogs, there is a vaccine against borreliosis). Ticks are a considerable health threat for humans; in addition to borreliosis, they can transmit the pathogen that causes encephalitis (FSME).

188. Toxoplasmosis: How can I tell whether my cat has toxoplasmosis?

In young cats, infection with the parasite *Toxoplasma gondii* can temporarily result in overall weakness and loss of appetite, while adult cats generally exhibit no symptoms of disease. The vet will examine your cat's feces to determine whether it is infected with the pathogen. Toxoplasmosis (see Info, page 120) in cats can readily be treated with medications.

189. Tumor: My cat has a little lump on its abdomen. How do I know whether it's benign or malignant?

Lumps and growths are known medically as tumors. Tumors can appear in any organ, singly or in numbers. They are more common in older cats than in young ones. Without a precise examination of the affected tissue, there is no way to tell for sure whether a tumor is benign or malignant. Generally, a benign tumor grows very slowly, does not infiltrate the surrounding tissue, and can be moved around under gentle pressure. A malignant growth rapidly increases in size, frequently also changes in shape, and tends to move (metastasize) to other tissue and organs, spreading via the bloodstream and lymphatic system. Tumors can be caused by external influences (environment, climate), by hereditary factors, by diet, and also by pathogens (such as a leukemia infection). Tumors on internal organs often go undiscovered until overall problems and functional disturbances appear. A growth or thickening involving a cat's skin or mammary glands, however, can be detected by the owner at an early stage, by regularly running your hands over the animal's body. If you can feel a knot, keep a close eye on it. Take your cat to the vet at once if there is any change in shape and size. Otherwise, show the vet the area during the next check-up or vaccination appointment. If there is any doubt, the vet will take a tissue sample and have it examined in the lab.

190. Urinary stones: **Can you prevent the formation of urinary stones?**

?

Lack of exercise, insufficient fluid intake (often in connection with dry food as the main item in the

---

INFO

Neutering
Surgical intervention under full anesthesia, in which the ovaries of a female cat or the testicles of a male cat are removed. Neutering prevents the female from becoming pregnant and protects her against uterine disease and tumors of the mammary glands. Castrated males generally discontinue their marking behavior. Unlike sterilization, neutering also prevents sexual behavior. The best time for neutering is onset of sexual maturity (female, at age of 6 months; male, at 8–10 months).

diet), and a genetic predisposition can contribute to formation of renal gravel and urinary stones. With gravel, the urine is mixed with pus and blood, and urination is difficult and very painful for the cat. Urinary stones can lead to a life-threatening blockage of the urethra (danger of kidney failure and bladder rupture). Tomcats are far more at risk than females because of the males' narrow urethra. If the cat is ill, the vet will attempt to evacuate the gravel or stone by irrigation, but with large stones usually only surgery can bring relief. Preventive measures include, first of all, plenty of exercise, a balanced diet, and consistent adherence to a special diet in the case of cats with an increased tendency to urinary stone formation (such as Persians). These steps sometimes will even cause already existing urinary stones to dissolve. In general, cats are especially prone to problems with urinary gravel. The umbrella term FLUTD (feline lower urinary tract disease) is applied to all illnesses of the cat's lower urinary tract.

191. Vaccination: With a live vaccine, is there any danger of infection for my cat?

In active immunization, the pathogens or certain pathogen components of the disease in question are administered, in order to stimulate the body's immune system to generate protective antibodies. Killed or live vaccines are injected. In the inactivated vaccine the pathogens have been killed, but in the live vaccine they are present in an altered or weakened form. Therefore the disease also cannot be triggered by the live vaccine. For a cat, the protective effect must be regularly renewed each year. The combination vaccines used for the inoculation offer protection against several diseases simultaneously. Passive immunization is performed with foreign antibodies. Unlike active immunization, where the protection provided must first develop, here it exists right after the inoculation, but is effective only for a few weeks.

192. Vaccination: Is a cat protected against infections immediately after vaccination?

After inoculation (active immunization), the body needs 2 to 3 weeks to produce the necessary antibodies and ensure complete immunity. The cat's basic vaccination includes initial and repeated inoculations, which are given with the exception of rabies shots at 3- to 4-week intervals (see Vaccination Schedule, page 106). Effective protection begins 2 weeks after the second vaccination. The annual boosters will close any gaps in your pet's immunity. To prevent feline distemper (FP), live vaccine is administered in a 2-year cycle.

193. Veterinary fees: How much can I expect to pay for veterinary care?

Being a responsible pet owner involves some basic expenses for supplies and medical care. If you can't afford these basic expenses, you should not take on the care of a cat. Veterinary fees will vary according to the geographic region in which you live. If you are considering getting a cat, scope out the prices in your area beforehand to determine whether you can afford a cat. Call your nearest vet's office (the one you would likely visit) and ask how much they charge for spaying or neutering a cat. This will be a one-time charge that likely will range from $60 (for neutering a male) to $125 (for spaying a female), depending on where

> **EXTRA TIP**
>
> **Pulse and respiration checks**
> A cat's pulse can most easily be taken on the inside of the upper thigh. At rest, a pulse of 120 to 140 beats per minute is normal. The breathing frequency of a healthy, relaxed cat is 20 to 40 breaths per minute, discernible by the rising and falling of the chest best measured by placing your hand on the chest.

you live. Many areas offer special low-cost spay-neuter programs. Contact your local humane society and ask if any such programs are available in your area. Also, some shelters alter kittens and cats before adopting them out, or they may arrange for discounted surgeries at your veterinarian's office. Another major veterinary cost you will incur is for annual health exams and vaccinations, which can range from approximately $60 to $100 for one cat. This, too, varies depending on where you live. There is no real way to tally approximate expenses for emergency trips to the vet and the cost of treating an illness or injury. You should, however, be financially prepared for such instances. You can also lessen the risk of your cat experiencing a costly illness or injury simply by keeping it safely indoors. The Web site at *http://cats.about.com/od/responsibleownership/ a/care_costs.htm* offers some useful information about the costs and responsibilities of cat ownership.

194. Vomiting: How seriously should I take it when my cat vomits?

Like diarrhea, vomiting can be triggered in cats by many different things, including food that is spoiled, spicy, too cold, or too hot, food intolerance, gastritis, ulcers, gallstones, diabetes, allergies, parasites, foreign objects in the stomach or esophagus, viral infections, and poisoning. The owner always needs to take action if the cat vomits continually or several times during a longer period, and if the vomiting is accompanied by other symptoms such as apathy, a rough coat, visible nictitating membranes, fever, refusal to eat, or diarrhea. Until the cause has been determined by the vet, you should not feed the cat. Always keep water available for it, however, to compensate for the loss of fluid through vomiting. Bringing up indigestible hairballs is a normal process, especially common during molting and in longhaired breeds.

195. Worm control: Should every cat be wormed regularly?

Worm infestation is not uncommon in house cats; almost 20% of adult animals and more than 90% of newborn kittens are infected with roundworm. Besides, roundworms, hookworms, and tapeworms are among the types most common in cats. Roundworms are transmitted via infected feces or mother's milk, while tapeworms are acquired from intermediate hosts like mice and fleas. Hookworms bore through the skin on the paws or are also passed on through the mother's milk. Since worms remove nutrients from the food, affected cats become visibly emaciated. Further, worm infestation can lead to poisoning and organ damage. When a cat is wormed, the worms are killed, but the medication also places the cat's organism under considerable stress. Therefore, indoor cats that never go out should be wormed only once a year or if there is justifiable suspicion. If there is none, having the vet check the feces is sufficient. If a flea infestation is present, however, once the fleas are under control, the cat must also be treated for tapeworms. Cats that go outdoors are at much greater risk of contracting worms, especially a tapeworm infection transmitted by captured prey. Generally they should be wormed one to four times a year, and worming should be done about 2 weeks before a scheduled vaccination. As an alternative to preventive worming, the vet also can perform regular fecal checks for cats that go outdoors and thus spare the animal the stress of the worming. Conscientious worm control in the case of kittens is indispensable, since almost all young cats have worms. Special hygiene and possibly more frequent examinations of the cat's feces are important if children live in your household and have close contact with cats.

ZOONOSES

Diseases that are communicable to humans by cats

DISEASE	SYMPTOMS IN A HUMAN
Rabies	Viral infection: affects primarily foxes. Vaccination of cat against rabies protects humans as well.
Catpox/cowpox	Viral infection: causes inflammations of the lymph nodes and poorly healing wounds.
Campylobacteriosis	Bacterial infection: leads to intestinal illnesses. Sources of infection are usually dogs, rarely cats.
Cat scratch disease (Bartonellosis)	Bacterial infection: usually transmitted to humans through bites and scratches. Course resembles flu infection, resulting in inflamed lymph nodes.
Pasteurellosis	Bacterial infection: transmitted through scratches and bites. Leads to abscesses, inflammation of lymph nodes and periosteum.
Salmonellosis	Bacterial infection: transmitted in direct contact, but also by infected feces. Mainly diarrhea.
Tuberculosis	Bacterial infection: now rare in cats.
Microsporia, trichophytia	Fungal infection (ringworm): communicated through direct contact, results in itching and patches on skin.
Giardiosis	Parasite infection: causes diarrhea and stomachache.
Toxoplasmosis	Parasite infection (see Info, page 120): risk for pregnant women and people with weakened immune systems.
Echinococcosis	Parasite infection (dog and fox tapeworm).
Toxocariasis	Parasite infection (roundworms): causes fever, coughing, and stomachache.

Anatomy and the Senses

This chapter describes a host of interesting details of the cat's external anatomy and amazing sensory abilities and explains what you, as a cat owner, need to pay special attention to.

196. Blindness: Our old tom is almost blind. Does that make life burdensome for him?

Although the eyes are the cat's most important sense organs, it can cope well with decreased vision and even with blindness, especially if the loss of sight is gradual and the cat is quite familiar with its environment. Many virtually blind cats move about so confidently in their accustomed surroundings that their owner may not even notice the impaired vision at all for quite some time. The cat's brain unfailingly stores all the topographical features of its home territory; even without visual feedback, it knows precisely how to get to its bed or to the litter box. Admittedly, this works only if everything in the household stays in its customary place and the furniture doesn't get rearranged. Since blind cats must rely on their ears, your tom's hearing should be checked, to make sure everything is all right. At close range, he gets his bearings primarily by means of his whiskers. If there is a second cat or a dog in the home, orientation will be easier for a blind cat. The sighted housemate then functions as a "seeing-eye dog" for the cat. The only thing your pet can't do anymore, of course, is go outdoors.

197. Coat color: On what genetic basis are coat colors and patterns inherited?

The chromosomes in the nucleus of every somatic cell of a living creature contain genes that carry hereditary information. Each gene determines a particular characteristic (such as coat color) or governs the functioning of organs or behaviors. The hereditary units for certain characteristics are passed on by both parents to their offspring. The genes do not mix but mold the observable physical characteristics (phenotype) of the next generation according to certain laws. In the process, individual genes win out over others; they express dominant inheritance, and always produce the same phenotypic effect. The weaker genes, inherited but producing no effect, are termed recessive. They affect the phenotype only if they are not overpowered by dominant characteristics. Thus, in a cat with the

genes for black coat color and for the tabby pattern
(the brindled or striped coat typical of feral cats), the
dominant tabby gene prevails over black. Individual
characteristics are also sex-linked, if the genes responsible for them are located on the sex chromosomes. In
contrast to the XX chromosome pair of a female, the
male has a dissimilar chromosome pair (XY). Thus,
for example, red coat color in a queen is always linked
to the X chromosome, so it can be transmitted only
once by the XY chromosome pair of a tom.

**198. Eye: Why is pupil size dependent on the light
conditions?**

What today is standard in cameras was "discovered"
for cats by evolution millions of years ago: automatic
aperture control. The pupil in a cat's eye adapts at
lightning speed to the changing light conditions from
a tiny opening in broad daylight to a completely
enlarged pupil in twilight. In the case of the domestic
cat and most other feline species, the pupil narrows to
a slit, while it is a dot-shaped opening in large cats
such as lions and tigers. The pupillary reflex makes
optimal vision possible even in unfavorable light conditions: In the dusk, a cat sees six times better than a
human. At the same time, the sensitive eye is perfectly
protected against incidence of strong light, so that the
cat can look directly into the sun without incurring
harm. The size of the pupil is governed by neural
impulses, and muscles in the iris are responsible for
making the adjustment. Further, the pupil of a cat's
eye is also a gauge of its mood: the pupil is greatly
enlarged in a cat that is afraid, normal in size in an
even-tempered animal, and narrowed when attacking
prey or when an enraged opponent is threatening.

**199. Eye color: Do odd-eyed cats have problems
seeing?**

Bi-colored eyes (in odd-eyed cats) are caused by an
anomaly in the pigmentation of the iris. This iris het-

erochromy is relatively common in cats (and in dogs). In odd-eyed cats, usually one eye is blue, and the other is brownish or copper-colored. Heterochromy can be hereditary, but it also can be caused by inflammation of the iris. The normally pigmented eye presents no problems with sight, but vision in the blue eye can be limited in twilight. It often lacks the tapetum lucidum, the light-reflecting layer at the back of the eye that refracts light rays and thus increases visual ability in dim light. To compensate for the lack of sensitivity to light, the pupil of a blue eye is more enlarged than that of a normal eye. This impairs visual acuity, and the eye reacts in a sensitive way to harsh light. The problems can be found in cats with either one or two blue eyes. If you shine light on a normal eye, it will be reflected by the tapetum as green. In an impaired blue eye, however, the pupil has a red gleam because the tapetum lucidum is absent and the light rays are reflected by the choroid. Typical in blue-eyed cats is a rapid, involuntary motion of the eyeball (nystagmus). With the oscillating motion, the eye is attempting to compensate for the lack of sensitivity and to get more light to the photoreceptors. In addition to impaired vision, white cats with blue eyes are often deaf.

200. **Field of vision: I'm continually amazed to see how accurately cats can jump. Do they learn this by constantly practicing?**

A cat's eyes point straight ahead so that the fields of vision overlap in a range of 130 degrees. In this zone, the cat sees things spatially. Stereoscopic vision is a precondition for gauging distances, for example, when attacking prey or getting ready for a leap onto the cornice. A cat has a 280-degree field of vision (a human's is only 210 degrees). Even without turning its head to one side, therefore, a cat is always informed about what is going on around it. Besides distance control, a perfect jumping technique also includes perfect body control. Here the tail plays an important role, because it functions as an automatic controller while the cat is airborne. And the fact that practice makes perfect, even for cats, is demonstrated by the practice jumps of young cat, which occasionally land offside.

201. Finding the way home: There are many stories about cats that found their way home after long wanderings. Are they just old wives' tales?

For cats, it's no problem to find the way back home from distances of 2 to 3 miles (3 to 5 km). In corresponding tests, most cats made their way straight home from the drop-off point even if they had been previously taken around on detours. Here cats with outdoor experience proved superior to indoor cats.

Scientists assume that in such wanderings a cat can resort to optical trail marks and acoustic images that are stored in its head in the form of an audiovisual memory. These may include, for example, the noise of a major highway, the ringing of bells in a church belfry, or the scream of a saw in a saw mill. In orientation, the strength and the direction of the sounds play a role, along with the site correlation of individual acoustic signals. In the attempts to find the way home, however, it also became clear that many cats go astray with distances in excess of 3 miles (5 km) and fail to reach home.

Thus, caution is called for in the case of reports of cats covering greater distances miles, not infrequently spending weeks or months on the road, finally to

INFO

Hearing mice

Mice are chatterboxes; they talk to each other nonstop. A human doesn't hear these high-frequency vocalizations, but a cat can register even tones of 70,000 Hz and is always tuned in to mouse radio. Here the ear flaps act as high-performance megaphones, and they can be directed independently of one another at a sound source. The eavesdropping operation works so perfectly that even blind cats with only the senses of hearing and touch can capture prey.

return home in more or less good shape. Familiar acoustic images and trail marks certainly play no role in these peregrinations. There are various attempts to explain the phenomena: Cats are said to be especially receptive to emissions and force fields, for example, to the earth's magnetic field or the differences in electrical charges in the atmosphere. Perhaps cats are also able to synchronize the position of the sun with their "internal clock," much as carrier pigeons do.

202. Flehmen response: A flehming cat seems to be in another world. What's going on with the animal?

The flehmen response is exhibited only by animals that have a Jacobson's organ (vomeronasal organ). Besides cats, they include horses, rhinoceroses, and snakes. The organ, located in a pair on the roof of the mouth, examines scents, especially those used in communication (pheromones). The scents are transferred through the tongue and special canals in the mouth. The scent analysis is accompanied by an unmistakable facial expression: A cat that is sniffing at the source of a scent holds its head erect, opens its mouth slightly, draws back the corners of its mouth, curls its upper lip, and wrinkles its nose. The reaction termed "flehmen" usually lasts for a few seconds. During this time, the flehming cat has an absent look, as if gazing into nothingness. The reaction to sexually enticing scents is especially pronounced. The flehmen response is seen especially in infatuated tomcats smelling the scent of queens in heat. Big cats such as lions exhibit this reaction more frequently than domestic cats.

In the flehmen response, the cat displays a typical grimace: slightly opened mouth, wrinkled nose, fixed gaze.

203. Hearing range: Why do cats react more strongly to high-pitched tones than to low ones?

The hearing range of a cat covers frequencies from 60 to about 70,000 Hz, and young cats can even hear sounds of 100,000 Hz. For comparison, humans hear in the range from about 16 to 20,000 Hz; dogs, 15–40,000 Hz. To hunt successfully, a cat must locate its prey as precisely as possible, not only optically but also acoustically. All the tones that matter most lie in the upper frequency range: They include, among other things, the scampering and rustling of mice and the squeaking and whispering by which the little rodents remain in contact with each others. The cat is always listening in on the same frequency.

204. Learning: How do cats learn?

For a cat, curiosity and the urge to discover are the most important incitements to learn about new

1 ⋁

2 ⋁

Mama as role model: On their outings together, little kittens learn by closely observing their mother.

Happy hunting: Through frequent practice, cats learn how to capture prey successfully and how to inflict the fatal bite properly.

things and acquire experience. If an experience proves to be positive and advantageous, it almost always is retained and then deepened and refined through experimentation and repetition. Unpleasant experiences, on the other hand, are rarely tried a second time. Learning on the basis of trial and error is often tedious and time-consuming. Learning by example is easier. Here the mother cat plays a major role. If she goes exploring with her offspring, the kittens observe very closely how she behaves in certain situations and especially toward humans. The more the mother does with her young, the better they cope with their environment. The apprenticeship continues once the kittens are eating independently and are no longer being nursed by their mother. For this reason, many breeders believe it is best to keep a kitten with its mother and littermates until it is at least 12 weeks old.

205. Littermates: How does it happen that the kittens in the same litter can look completely different?

Fighting among males has no influence on who finally wins the battle for the female's favors. The decision is made by the queen alone, by assuming the mating position, her body pressed flat to the ground and her tail held to one side as she makes treading movements with her hind legs and presents her rear end, held high in the air, to the tom of her choice. A female that is ready to mate will allow herself to be served by several males if she has the opportunity. The kittens in a litter can certainly have different fathers and be quite different in appearance.

Together, we're strong: Littermates that grow up together develop more courage and self-confidence.

206. Perception of sound: **Why can cats sleep even in a noisy environment?**

Cats' ears are high-performance sound receivers. In terms of its ability to hear and to locate sounds, a cat is superior to a human: When young, we can hear tones up to 20,000 Hz (with increasing age, the upper limit drops noticeably), while the upper hearing range of an adult cat is 70,000 Hz (dog: 40,000 Hz) and that of a young cat is even higher: 100,000 Hz. With respect to the level of sound, too, we are no match: A noise that we register only with difficulty is picked up by a cat even at an intensity 1,000 times lower. To keep from being totally confused by the countless noises that reach its ear from all sides, it employs a skill that we can only dream of: It can selectively tune out. All the tones that have no meaning for the cat are filtered out, and only especially interesting noises are further processed. Thanks to this selective hearing, a cat can even take a nap in noisy surroundings, provided that the sound background is familiar to it. It is instantly wide awake, however, when certain key stimuli reach its ear—such as the shrill squeaking by which mice communicate among themselves (so-called contact calls), which are inaudible to the human ear.

207. Place memory: **My cat registers every change in its surroundings. Is this important to her?**

The cat has an infallible place memory and remembers the position of objects in its living area so precisely that it could find its way around even with its eyes closed. It is even able to visualize in detail the topography of the terrain or of a residence just by seeing it from the outside, without investigating it more closely. The significance of this ability is obvious: If you know exactly what is where, you register every change and are safe from potential unwelcome surprises. For a cat, the position of an object is also linked with a certain meaning. If the object changes its place, it loses the previous significance. In daily practice this can cause problems; for example, if the litter box is moved to another place and is no longer found acceptable.

208. Righting reflex: Does a falling cat always land on its feet?

As it falls, a cat rolls in midair: This righting reflex ensures that its upper body turns toward the ground first, and then the lower body follows. In this rotation, the tail assumes a controlling function and stabilizes the position once the sense of equilibrium signals that the body is normally oriented. The cat lands on all fours. This works, however, only if there is enough time to execute the turning maneuver completely. When falling from heights of less than 10 feet (3 m), cats not infrequently land on their backs and incur serious injuries, while in a fall from a great height the legs can no longer break the impact.

209. Seeing colors: Do cats see the world in the same colors as we do?

The cat, like the dog, was long considered colorblind. Today we know that cats see their world roughly the same way as a human with red/green colorblindness. The light-sensitive sensory cells are located in the retina of the eye: Rod cells react to differences in brightness, and cones react to colors. The human eye has three types of cones—for blue, green, and red, which provide us with trichromatic color vision. The cat like most other mammals has only two cone types in its eye: for blue and green (dichromatic color vision). Thus the cat's eye has virtually no receptivity for red, orange, and the corresponding shades in between.

The color vision functions well only with relatively large color fields; smaller ones are perceived by a cat only as gradations of gray. For a cat, which is active at dusk and at night, the light-sensitive rods are far more important than the cone cells. Therefore, the retina of the cat's eye is equipped with a disproportionately large number of rods, and for reasons of space alone there are comparatively few cones.

210. Seeing in dim light: Why do a cat's eyes glow in the dark when you shine a light on them?

In dim light, the cat's eye works on the principle of a low-light amplifier. The incident light activates the sensory cells and then strikes the tapetum lucidum, a reflective layer at the back of the eye, which reflects it to the sensory cells and thus activates them a second time. Through this dual use of the light, the light yield increases by a factor of 1.4, and the cat easily can get its bearings optically, even in semi-darkness. In total darkness, however, even the cat can see nothing. The tapetum lucidum consists mainly of guanine crystals and is found in the choroid membrane. It also provides other vertebrates, such as horses, foxes, dogs, cattle, and deer, with good night vision. The reflection of the light causes cats' eyes with normal pigmentation to look green in the dark when light flashes at or shines on them.

211. Seeing movement: When I stand motionless, my cat can't detect me at greater distances. What is the reason for this?

Cats go out stalking at twilight. In these difficult conditions, the cat's eye proves its high capability. The good vision in low light is offset by reduced visual acuity, which is seven to ten times less than that of a human. The cat's eyesight is keenest at a range of 65 to 20 feet (2 to 6 m), precisely where it normally gets its prey in its sights. Unmoving objects are seen by a

A cat doesn't miss anything that moves in its vicinity. Its field of vision covers an area of 280 degrees.

cat unclearly or are completely overlooked. A mouse that stops in its tracks often escapes with its life—not least of all also because when stalking, a cat's sense of smell plays only a secondary role. On the other hand, even the slightest movements don't escape a cat, even if they take place at the outermost edge of its field of vision. Also irrelevant is how far away they are from the cat: Just take a few steps or gesture with your hand, and your cat will immediately know it's you.

212. Sense of equilibrium: How does a cat manage to balance safely on a railing scarcely as wide as one of its paws?

Cats are born with the faculty for climbing and balancing. To employ the technique correctly, however, it

> *Targeted flight: The tail is used to steer when jumping and ensures that the cat lands safely on all fours.*

takes plenty of practice. Young cats start these activities at the age of only 6 or 7 weeks, trying to walk on tree trunks and exploring roofs and balconies. These activities are not without danger. Often enough, the youngsters take on more than they can handle, since their body control is not yet as perfect as that of an older cat. Especially when they are balancing, a physical flaw can be observed: Adult cats use the tail as a major balancing aid, much in the same way they use it to steer when jumping. The thin "rattail" of young cats is not a big help, and more than once they experience rough landings. By watching a Manx or a Cymric, you can see just how important the tail is in such activities: The tail-less purebred cats can hardly maintain their balance. A problem that troubles many humans in the air is nonexistent for a cat in its artistic high-wire feats: Whether a cat is 6 or 60 feet (2 or 20 m) above the ground, it never gets dizzy.

> **INFO**
>
> **Genetics**
> Genetics deals with the mechanisms by which hereditary characteristics are produced and transmitted by parents to their offspring. Besides classical genetics, molecular genetics plays a central role today. It analyzes the processes of heredity on the basis of the molecular structures that carry genetic information (deoxyribonucleic acid, DNA).

213. Sense of heat: My tom lies in the sun until his coat almost gets burned. Doesn't he sense the heat?

Some cats permit themselves to sunbathe until you involuntarily draw back when you touch their hot coats. Even black cats have no problem with sunshine and summer temperatures. Cats like warmth and tolerate it as well: While a human no longer feels comfortable once the temperature of the skin reaches 81°F (44°C), cats don't need to cool off until their skin

THE CAT'S SENSES

SENSORY ABILITY	DESCRIPTION
Sight	The cat is an eye-minded creature. It has a 180-degree field of vision, and in the central range it sees spatially. Cats' eyes react especially to movement, and color vision plays a secondary role. The tapetum lucidum improves the cat's ability to see in dim light.
Hearing	Cats' ears are receptive to high-frequency tones (hearing range up to 70,000 Hz) in particular. The ear flaps can be directed at a sound source independently of one another.
Smell	Smells are of great significance in communication, for example, when cats greet each other and use scent to mark. Food is not touched unless it has passed the smell test.
Touch	Pressure receptors in the balls of the feet detect vibrations, and the facial vibrissae (whiskers and other tactile hairs) react to every movement and measure the width of boltholes.
Taste	The taste buds on the tongue distinguish salty, sour, and bitter tastes. The cat cannot taste sweet things.
Equilibrium	Cats have a well-developed sense of equilibrium. In freefall, a righting reflex ensures that a cat lands on its feet. In balancing, the tail maintains equilibrium.
Time	Its unerring sense of time enables the cat to keep to a fixed schedule while performing many activities.

temperature exceeds 126°F (52°C). Although heat and cold receptors are distributed all over the body, it sometimes takes an amazingly long time for a cat to notice that it's really too hot on top of the radiator or that it has just singed its fur. In addition to the sense of smell, the sense of warmth is the only one already developed in a newborn kitten. The heat receptors next to its nose tell the blind, deaf little creature where its mother and littermates are, so it can snuggle close to them and store vital warmth. Cats retain their love of warmth all their lives. Nevertheless, on hot days always reserve a place in the shade for your pet as well. In addition, never leave a cat closed up in a car on a hot day because temperatures inside the car can reach life-threatening levels and cause heat stroke.

214. Sense of smell: Is it true that the sense of smell is less important for cats than for dogs?

The dog is a so-called macrosmate; it lives primarily in a world of smells. The anatomy of the canine nose is evidence of this as well: The olfactory mucosa of a dachshund is 11 in.² (75 cm²) in size, and that of a German shepherd, 30 in.² (200 cm²). The number of olfactory cells is 125 million and 200 million, respectively. A cat's olfactory mucosa totals 3 in.² (20 cm²), with 60 million olfactory cells, while humans have barely 0.7 in.² (5 cm²) and 20 million olfactory cells.

Cats get their bearings primarily optically, but odors play an important role for them too. The sense of smell is already highly developed in a newborn kitten, while its eyes and ears are still shut. It is smell alone that draws them to the milk in the teats. Only at the age of 3 weeks do their eyes become their most important sense organ. Nevertheless, scents continue to be a major factor in determining feline behavior: Food is always subjected to a smell check before it is consumed; in conspecific communication it is the nose check that is the chief determinant of whether they can stand each other. Cats impregnate objects, other animals, but also familiar humans with scents by rubbing their head and flanks against them. Cats leave scent messages when they mark with feces and leave scratches, and sexual behavior too is stimulated by attractants. Only when hunting does a cat rely solely on its eyes and ears.

215. Sense of time: What is the "internal clock" all about?

Like many other mammals, cats have an infallible sense of time. Scientists assume that behaviors, metabolic processes, and other physiological procedures are controlled by an "internal clock" in a roughly 24-hour (circadian) rhythm. With birds, researchers have identified a link between remembering time and the release of the hormone melatonin. For cats, the "clock in the head" has great significance: In many of their activities, they adhere to a fixed schedule; this applies to mealtimes as well as to going stalking in their territory and taking a morning nap (see Tip, page 172). Cats that jointly use certain paths along the borders of their territory make their rounds at different times, to avoid getting in each other's way.

216. Sense of touch: Is it true that cats have special tactile organs in the balls of their paws?

The Pacini corpuscles (named for the Italian anatomist Filippo Pacini) found in the foot pads are tiny sensory organs that react to touch and can detect

---

INFO

Psi phenomena
The Greek letter psi is used to refer to events and reactions for which no logical explanation can be found. Some scientists are convinced that cats possess abilities that are beyond our power to imagine, and that they can, for example, anticipate that a familiar human is about to have an accident, fall ill, or die and are also able to warn us of threatening emergency situations such as epileptic seizures.

shock waves and vibrations. The Pacini corpuscles are so sensitive that even the scurrying of a passing mouse does not escape them. It has long been known that cats, like many other animals, register an impending earthquake many hours before humans. The paws play a central role here, since they obviously can detect even the tiniest tremors.

217. Sexual maturity: When does a cat mature?

Most females undergo puberty between the sixth and eighth months of life, while males mature somewhat later (by about the tenth month). There are females and males that are definitely late bloomers, as well as animals that mature early. Females of some breeds may go into heat when only 5 or 6 months old. Physical development, however, does not end with the onset of puberty: Generally cats are fully grown at 15 months, some breeds not until 18 or 20 months of age.

218. Sweating: Are cats really unable to sweat?

Cats can sweat, though unlike us, they do not perspire all over. Their sweat glands are located between the balls of the feet, at the corners of the chin, beside the lips, and by the anus. Moreover, cats are relatively insensitive to high temperatures: Their coat can reach a temperature of over 92°F (50°C) without any harm. On a hot day, a cat uses its tongue to spread saliva throughout its coat, and the evaporation has a cooling effect. A cat also sweats when it is excited or gets panicky. Then the sweaty paws leave damp marks, and the sweetish odor of sweat can be detected even by a human nose.

219. Tongue: Which flavors can a cat's tongue distinguish?

A cat also subjects its food to a scent check first, and the fatty odor of the meat is of primary importance here. In comparison to the nose, the tongue plays a subordinate role. The similarity between the olfactory cells of the nose and the taste receptors on the tongue, however, shows that taste and smell are connected. The cat's tongue can tell the difference between bitter and salty and sour, but it cannot taste sweet things. Amazingly, it also has special taste buds that are receptive to water.

220. Walking on tiptoes: How are cats able to walk around so quietly?

Unlike a human, who like bears and apes flexes the entire hand or foot surface when walking, a cat touches only the tips of its fingers and toes to the ground. The pad cushions, protected by thick skin, act as shock absorbers when a cat jumps and enable it to move almost noiselessly. The retractable claws do not touch the ground when the cat walks. Young kittens still have a hard time keeping their balance, and until the third week of life they put their entire foot to the ground. Only then do they gradually develop the ability to walk on tiptoes.

EXTRA TIP

Keeping appointments
Cats don't just go about their lives in a random way; they perform their activities and duties in accordance with a fixed schedule. This applies to checking out their territory and taking a nap, as well as to mealtimes and playtimes. And they also expect their human to keep agreed-upon appointments: for feeding, playing, and cuddling and for promptly coming home from the office. If you repeatedly appear too late or forget appointments altogether, you run the risk of huffy rejection, protest, and more.

221. Whiskers: What purpose do the whiskers serve?

The whiskers on the upper lip and the other long hairs on a cat's face (above the eyes and on the chin and cheeks) are known as vibrissae. Vibrissae are tactile hairs, which react to the slightest touch. They enable the cat to find its way in the dark, measure the width of boltholes, and provide additional information about a conspecfic during the nose-to-nose greetings typical of felines. When touched, the tactile hairs on the forehead ensure that the eyes close reflexively and are protected against injury. At the root of a whisker are found four different types of sensory cells, which transmit an abundance of data to the individual parts of the brain for processing. During hunting, too, the vibrissae are indispensable. The cat delivers the fatal bite when its tactile hairs touch the prey, and when it is carrying a mouse the whiskers monitor the position of the animal between the teeth and any changes in that position.

Language and Behavior

This chapter answers all your questions about a cat's behavior and way of communicating. If you understand the most important forms of feline behavior and the concepts of the language of cats, you can become better acquainted with your pet and succeed in avoiding problems.

222. Aggressiveness: When cuddling, my cat often starts to scratch and bite out of a clear blue sky. Can I break my pet of this habit?

In cats, a bite inhibition ensures that no serious injuries are caused, even in fierce play-fighting. The bite inhibition is innate, but must still be practiced by a young cat. When playing with its littermates, a kitten learns what is permissible and where its playmates will put up a loud protest. The mother cat, too, does not wear kid gloves in such matters of kitten-rearing; hissing and swatting hard with her paws, she trounces the little ruffians when they get seriously out of line. Cats that have been separated from mother and littermates too early lack this experience, and their manners frequently leave much to be desired as their human playmate realizes with some pain. Here's how to train your cat to play gently: Stop the game if it bites or scratches. As a reprimand, a sharp "No!" and a little tap on its nose are sufficient. Don't resume play until the cat is calm again. And no play-fighting with cats that extend their claws during the game. Long-sleeved clothing will protect children against getting scratched. Break off the game at once if the cat expresses its displeasure by raising a paw in warning, twitching its tail, and putting its ears back. Pet and praise your cat at the end of the play hour.

223. Anal display: What is meant by a cat's anal display?

The mutual sniffing of the anal region, in addition to making nose contact, is part of feline greeting behavior. The individual scent given off by the anal glands located next to the opening of the anus tells just who a cat is dealing with. It depends on a cat's level of self-confidence whether it allows every strange conspecific to see its anal region. Animals that are friends frequently dispense with sniffing each other's rear ends and limit themselves to a rather sketchy nose contact.

224. Apathy: Our 11-year-old tom often sits lethargically in a corner. Is this a sign of aging?

You should take your cat's apathetic behavior seriously. Lethargy is often a symptom of illness, especially if accompanied by physical indications such as a rough coat, discharge from the eyes and mouth, or a continuously visible nictitating membrane. In an older cat, it is often problems with bones and joints (arthrosis) that limit a cat's mobility, but they rarely cause it to seem apathetic. If no disease is found to be present, you need to look for the causes of the unusual behavior in your domestic environment. Cats are creatures of habit, and depending on their disposition they react to changes by displaying protest, aggressiveness, noncompliance, or withdrawal into lethargy. Possible triggers: loss of a caregiver, neglect, "jealousy" of a new member of the family (infant, owner's new spouse or life partner, second cat), boredom, oppression by dominant members of their species. Usually the apathy is resolved only when the situation is cleared up or at least alleviated. Attention and activity are especially important in this phase. Even if the cat doesn't immediately participate, it needs the feeling that it continues to be Number One in your life. A rambunctious little kitten, too, can sometimes help senior felines find a new zest for life.

225. Arching its back: Why does a cat arch its back when it's afraid?

The cat's arched back is a sign of the conflict the cat is in: The situation is anything but safe for it, and actually it would prefer to flee, but it is also not sure whether it would escape unscathed. So it makes a virtue of necessity, puts on a show of strength despite all its fear, and threatens its opponent (fear-related aggression). This contradictory state of mind also produces the typical arching of the back: While the hind legs maintain their position and don't give an inch, the front legs want to give in and are retracted, which necessarily results in a contorted body. The cat stands sideways on stiffened legs and raises the hair on its back and tail.

226. Bird hunting: Do housecats endanger the songbird population?

Almost three fourths of the offspring of our songbirds die young. Their numbers are decimated by hunger, cold, disease, and parasites. But Mother Nature planned ahead and regulated the reproduction of birds to compensate for these high rates of loss. The songbird population, therefore, is not in danger. The few birds that are caught by cats make no material difference here. In thousands of X-rays, the stomachs of cats of different origins were found to contain skeletal remains of birds in only a few instances. When cats can catch birds at all, they generally get only weakened and sick ones; a healthy bird is an absolute exception. Finally, by hunting rats, cats even contribute to lowering the risks for the population of ground-breeding bird species because their nests are robbed primarily by rats.

227. Bite inhibition: My 8-month-old tomcats tussle like wildcats and bite each other. Can they hurt each other?

While playing, young cats try out behavioral patterns and sequences of movements that will be important for them later on, particularly attack, defense, and prey capture. The playful nature of the actions is shown by the fact that, in comparison with a real case of emergency, they are performed in an exaggerated way and look especially ferocious. Nevertheless, nobody gets hurt. That is guaranteed by an innate bite inhibition. It needs some practice, however. The necessary feedback is provided by the loudly protesting playmates if the sharp little teeth should ever get too far under their skin. Later the cat has to learn to overcome its bite inhibition in order to be successful with real prey. Owing to lack of hunting practice, however, many indoor cats never manage to do that.

228. Bristling: Do cats raise their bristles only when they're afraid?

By bristling, a cat changes its body outline and seems larger. This is an innate capability. A frightened animal causes all its hair to stand erect, while a threatening animal bristles only certain areas (back, tail). In cold weather, too, a cat's coat gets puffier. The cushion of air in the bristled coat insulates and guards against heat loss. With longhaired cats, erection of the hair (piloerection) is hardly noticeable.

229. Brotherhood: Do the mysterious brotherhoods of tomcats really exist?

The term "brotherhood of tomcats" was coined by ethologist Paul Leyhausen, who studied feline behavior. He uses it to describe the loose association of males in a residential neighborhood. Within the "men's league," things usually are peaceful, and the hierarchical battles follow a ritualized pattern and are less serious than true confrontations between rival cats. Males that are new to the neighborhood must first prove themselves in combat before they are accepted. Toms are less

INFO

Preening behavior in cats
Cats are some of the cleanliest animals in existence, and they set aside several hours a day for grooming their coat and body. Most of the work is done by the tongue, which serves as washcloth, curry comb, and comb in one. Wherever it can't reach, the dampened back of a paw can wash. The incisors assist with coat and claw care. Among feline friends, mutual coat grooming performs a social function. Kittens make their first preening attempts when only a few weeks old.

> *When playing, things get pretty rough some-
> times. But the young cat's attack obviously
> does not go down particularly well.*

territory-bound than queens. The brotherhood too has
no fixed territory, but oversees a larger area of activity
in which its members take action against intruders or
go out hunting for females. Associations of toms, as
well as differently structured leagues of queens, are
found primarily in southern countries with a large percentage of strays. For these brotherhoods, the search
for food usually has top priority.

**230. Catfights: Toms often really get into a scrap.
Can they do each other serious harm?**

Only a few old warriors are really looking for trouble.
Most toms try to stay out of each other's way or to

make an orderly retreat when a chance encounter occurs, without losing face in the process. But if combat does result, they fight with no holds barred, and the story not infrequently has a bloody ending. Bites and scratches are inflicted. Numerous notches on the ears and grazed nose leather are indications of the risks incurred by battle-tried toms. Feline Immunodeficiency Virus (FIV) is spread through bites received primarily in fighting. That's why it's important to vaccinate cats that go outside.

Especially at risk are the eyes, where a well-placed blow from a paw with extended claws can have bad results. The long incisors inflict deep bites that easily become infected and not infrequently result in an abscess that is slow to heal. If the toms are really tangled together, they usually try to bite each other's elbows. If a male comes home with obvious battle scars and has scratches and bites, you always should take him to the vet when in doubt.

231. "Chattering:" Why does a cat chatter or bleat when it sees birds outside the window?

When a cat sees a prey animal that it can't reach, it opens its mouth slightly and, quickly moving its lower jaw up and down, emits greatly muted tones that sound like chattering or bleating. It doesn't take its eyes off the object of its desire for an instant, it crouches in preparation for a leap, and the twitching

INFO

Hunting behavior of a predator
Take advantage of every cover and sneak up as close as possible: The cat attacks prey only from a short distance and waits a long while to get in an advantageous position. Nevertheless, it often fails and has to go away empty-handed. Animals such as rats, which put up a fight against the feline hunter, however, do not fit into the prey-catching pattern. And a cat also can do nothing with a mouse that scurries right across its feet.

tail betrays great excitement. This curious behavior can be readily observed in cats that see a bird through a closed window. The meaning of the sound produced is unclear.

232. Claw sharpening: Does a cat need to sharpen its claws on a regular basis?

During the process of claw sharpening, the old claw sheaths or parts of them are removed and the claws themselves are honed. For this purpose, the cat uses a coarse surface that it can dig the claws into: outdoors, usually tree bark, indoors, a sisal-wrapped scratching post or a coconut-fiber mat. The claws on the hind legs are not sharpened, but are gnawed at with the teeth and cleaned. Many cats are peculiar about where they scratch: Outdoors, they generally use certain trees, on which the work of the claws often is visible from a distance, and indoors too there are favorite scratching places; sometimes, despite the availability of a luxury-model scratching post, these unfortunately include expensive rugs and designer sofas. Sharpening claws in the presence of other cats is a typical gesture meant to impress. Moreover, scents obviously are also deposited when a cat sharpens its claws. Claw sharpening is part of the cat's species-specific expressive behavior, and the opportunity for it must be available at all times. This possibility is denied it by surgical removal of the claws, which is permitted in the United States but prohibited in others.

Claw sharpening has two purposes: claw grooming and marking. Unfortunately, sometimes a cat also uses places that are off limits.

233. Comfort behaviors: What is meant by the term comfort behaviors?

What we have discovered as "wellness" is something cats have known about for a long time: ways of behaving that promote relaxation and well-being and keep the circulatory system and metabolism up to speed.

Comfort behaviors include cleaning and washing the skin and coat, rubbing on objects, and claw grooming, as well as sunbathing and stretching to loosen the muscles. Feline comfort behavior also has an important social meaning, as when animals that are friends lick each other, usually in places their own tongues can't reach. Licking the coat of dominant conspecifics serves to placate and helps defuse a tense situation. Here the act is performed by the lower-ranking cat alone and is not reciprocated.

234. Compulsive behavior: How can I get our cat to stop chasing its tail?

Compulsive behavior such as constantly chasing its own tail usually has psychological causes, such as boredom, separation anxiety, or oppression by another cat. If the behavioral stereotype develops a momentum of its own, it often is retained for a long time. A lasting remedy is found only when the cause is identified and eliminated. Play with your cat regularly and offer it other kinds of activity to distract it. Compulsive actions such as continuous scratching and excessive licking can cause self-inflicted damage and lead to serious health problems.

235. Dance of relief: Why do cats frequently jump wildly around their prey?

When hunting, a cat is under great tension, and it has to repeatedly overcome its fear, not only where animals that are fit to fight, such as rats, are concerned. After the capture, the cat lets out its pent-up excitement in a dance of relief, jumping wildly in circles around its prey. The release of tension often seems so important, even to very hungry cats, that they put off satisfying their hunger. A mouse that has survived the attack relatively unharmed or is playing dead will quite often take advantage of the cat's self-absorbed dance of relief to escape to safety. When playing with prey objects such as a toy mouse or piece of crumpled paper, too, cats offer such "dance interludes."

236. Defecation site: Why do cats neglect to bury their feces in some sites?

The instinct to bury the stool and leave no telltale smells ensures that a cat can be depended on to use its litter box. Outdoors, too, it usually carefully covers the feces with soil, sand, or leaves. At some places in the terrain, however, the cat leaves its feces uncovered, almost as if it had forgotten its inborn cleanliness. But this behavior has nothing to do with soiling; rather, its purpose is like that of marking by spraying urine. Here it serves primarily to document its own rights of ownership: The defecation sites are located next to and atop prominent terrain features along the cat's territorial boundaries and thus are a kind of warning and information sign for passing felines.

237. Displacement behavior: What do cats do in conflict situations?

In a conflict situation, it is hard to decide on a certain behavior or action. Cats not infrequently get into such a situation in a confrontation with conspecifics or other animals. If the cat can't spontaneously decide on fight or flight, it exhibits displacement and reacts in a way that is inappropriate to the situation and does not fulfill its actual biological function. A typical displacement behavior for a cat is excessive licking, which is comparable with a human's awkward reaction of head-scratching.

238. Dominance: Does a cat suffer when it lives with dominant members of its species?

Hierarchical distinctions can be observed even among kittens. They are stamped by their personality structure and, to a large extent, also by their early association with humans. Among littermates that grow up together, life-long friendships often develop. In the rare instances when puberty is followed by dominance problems and territorial squabbling, neutering is a remedy. Living together can be more difficult when a new cat joins the household. The owner of the territory is basically in a stronger position and asserts its territorial claims, usually in a way that cannot be overlooked. If the cat retains its attitude of rejection for a lengthy period and seriously oppresses the intimidated newcomer, you will have to find the second cat a new home to spare it long-term stress. If conflict arises only at certain flashpoints, however, the owner often can defuse the situation with patience and skill, for example, by providing several places to nap and separate feeding areas. When keeping three or more cats, disequilibrium often results because some will form an alliance and confront another. Since a home is unlikely to offer suitable opportunities for retreat, the owner has to intervene here too, before the outnumbered cat becomes ill from intense stress.

239. Dreaming: Can cats dream?

Like humans, cats dream in so-called REM sleep, characterized by rapid eye movements under the closed lids. These sleep phases usually can be identified by the twitching of the whiskers, mouth, and paws. Obviously, the cat is processing the day's experiences at these times and, as its gentle meowing indicates, some of them were pretty exciting events. Cats spend up to two-thirds of the day asleep. Longer phases of light sleep alternate with short phases of deep sleep. It is assumed that deep sleep serves primarily to regenerate the body after the stresses of the growth stage. A cat quickly wakes from light sleep, but much stronger stimuli are needed to rouse it from deep sleep.

240. Eating behavior: A dog gulps its food, a cat eats unhurriedly. What causes the difference?

As a pack animal, a dog is rarely alone, even when eating, and has to be constantly on its guard lest other dogs try to make off with the best bits. Rapid swallowing of the food is the safest way to prevent food from being stolen. This inherited behavior is deep-seated, even though most family dogs have long had no need to fear that other canines are looking enviously at their dinner. The cat, as a loner, has things easier, since it need not fear any undesirable meal-sharers. Whereas a dog makes hardly any effort to check the smell or taste of its food, a cat is far pickier: If the food is too hot or too cold or unable to pass the smell test, cats will do an about-face and go away insulted. And you can tell right away whether it tasted good: After a tasty meal, the cat will lick and wash itself thoroughly. Some cats leave a few morsels in the bowl for the sake of politeness. That is an indication that they are full and want to save the rest for later.

241. Facial expressions: You can tell from my cat's face whether it is feeling up to par or not. Can other cats read its expression too?

Cats have a highly developed, complex body language and set of vocalizations (see overview, page 194). During communication, several individual linguistic elements are usually interlinked to produce a certain unmistakable verbal image. Facial expression is used especially to communicate at close range. A cat's face is extraordinarily versatile and signals an animal's intentions, demands, and mood unmistakably, depending on the position and expression of the mouth, forehead, nose, eyes, ears, and whiskers. Cats are even able to adjust their language precisely to a conversational partner, and then they only use the half of their face and body that is turned toward the person being addressed for communicating, while the other side remains neutral. The tip of a cat's nose, as it were, tells conspecifics whether the animal is looking for trouble, wants to keep its distance, or is coming with friendly intentions.

242. Fear: When company comes, my kitten disappears under the armoire. How can I bolster its self-confidence?

Being shy with strangers usually has its roots in infancy, if cats are kept isolated and have scarcely any contact with humans and other cats. Pampered cats, cats fixated on their owner, and cats that have had bad experiences with humans also keep their distance. Fear is deep-seated, and things that were neglected in kittenhood will mold behavior for a long time. A practical tip: Take the kitten on your lap and ask someone the cat doesn't know to enter the room without knocking. Pet the kitten all the while and talk to it softly, but don't hold it on your lap against its will. Offer the visitor a chair and chat with him or her without bothering any further about the cat. In the

All eyes and ears: The cat is wide-awake and focused, but the facial expression indicates that it feels a bit uneasy about things.

Final warning: There's a storm approaching, but the large pupils and laid-back ears also signal uncertainty.

Most cats really dislike getting wet, but they all are enthusiastic about playing with drops of water.

first few meetings, it will continue to hide right away. Repeat the exercise until the cat notices that the stranger doesn't intend to do it any harm.

243. Fear of water: Are all cats afraid of water?

Cats have a schizophrenic relationship to water. Only a few enjoy a full bath, but all cats like to play with drops of water (from a faucet, for example). Many go out stalking in rain and snow and accept the wet feet, and some prove to be passionate anglers, able to skillfully use their paws to catch fresh fish from the edge of a body of water. All cats can swim, but only specialists like the Turkish Van voluntarily go in the water.

244. Greeting ritual: Why do cats sniff each other, nose to nose?

When encountering other members of their species, cats engage in nose-to-nose contact. They stand so close that their noses almost touch. The scent check and movements of the whiskers (see page 173) give the cat a picture of its conspecific. Additional information is exchanged during mutual sniffing of rear ends. Cats that are well acquainted usually just hint at the greeting ritual and dispense with the extensive inspection. Cats also use this form of greeting for other animals and for humans. With familiar humans and animals, rubbing their flanks and offering their heads for caressing also play an important role as proof of affection, with scents being transmitted in the process.

245. Grieving: Our two toms were never friends. Nevertheless, the younger one seemed upset after the death of his housemate. Was he grieving?

How accustomed cats cat grow to one another and though they never show it openly how much they value the presence of the other cat is frequently apparent only after one of them is gone. Depending on its disposition, the "bereaved" partner reacts with confusion and wanders restlessly through the house or withdraws, sits lethargically in a corner, and stares into space. Others tend to roam and vanish for days. During this phase, the cat needs plenty of attention and affection.

During the greeting ritual, cats sniff each other nose to nose. Animals that are friends frequently dispense with this scent check.

This too is part of cats' way of greeting each other: Thorough sniffing of the rear end tells just who you're dealing with.

246. Hiding places: **Why does my cat creep into all the cupboards, chests, and pockets?**

Cavelike places, cracks, cupboard drawers, suitcases, and cardboard boxes have an almost magical power to attract cats. Responsible for this strong desire to slip through narrow openings, as well as for the cat's pronounced curiosity and urge to explore, is probably the search for suitable places to hide and nap. Cat caves offer retreat and a sense of security and are especially interesting if the cat, while in concealment, can look out and observe its surroundings.

247. Hierarchy: **Is there a fixed hierarchy among cats?**

Positions of rank are less obvious among cats than among dogs. On the other hand, even when kittens play, they try to be the one who sets the tone. Generally, extroverted and physically skillful kittens develop into dominant cats. Here, early association with humans plays an important role, in addition to inherited personality characteristics. Introverted kittens often remain shy and mistrustful all their lives. Toward its conspecifics, a cat employs certain gestures of dominance to underscore its status, such as claw sharpening. Neutering will eliminate many problems of dominance.

248. High perches: **Why do cats prefer elevated places to rest and sit?**

Height offers a cat decisive advantages: From the elevated observation points (observatories) in its territory, no change escapes the cat, and it is immediately on the spot if an unwelcome conspecific shows up in the area it occupies and defends. In confrontations, too, the party in the higher position has a better deal and is a match even for better opponents. Indoors, a scratching post with caves and platforms on several levels will be accepted as enthusiastically as a box seat in the bookcase. Suitable climbing aids are ropes, little stairs, and ladders. If you want to offer your pet something special, build it a walkway that runs through your home near the ceiling.

249. Hunting behavior: **What triggers the hunting instinct?**

The cat's prey-capturing behavior is innate (see Info, page 181). It is triggered by acoustic and optical key stimuli, including the scurrying and rustling noises and the squeaks with which mice communicate (contact calls), and all small objects that move away quickly. Generally a cat relies on its eyes when catching prey, but it also can rely on its hearing alone. In delivering the fatal bite, the facial tactile hairs have a control function. The sense of smell plays no role in hunting. The hunting instinct does not depend on whether the cat is full or hungry. Quite a few cat owners feed their mouse hunters very generously, trying in this way to keep them from constantly dragging captured mice into the house. And they accomplish the exact opposite: First, a full tummy doesn't dissuade a cat from hunting, and second, a well-nourished cat usually is especially fit and has more luck as a hunter.

EXTRA TIP

Talking to your cat
➤ Talk to your cat in a quiet, soft voice and pay attention to its reactions (see Cat Language, page 194).
➤ Squat down when you make contact with your pet. That's the only way you can read its facial expression.
➤ Don't try to persuade a cat to cooperate if it is sleepy or hungry.
➤ A cat is attentive only in its familiar environment, where it is not distracted by strange noises and smells.

250. Hunting instinct: **My tom is visibly frustrated when a mouse gets away from him. Can such failures put a damper on his urge to hunt?**

Cats are skilled hunters. Nevertheless, success is frequently denied them, and only one of every four pursuits ends in prey capture. The flops, however, in no way impair their hunting instinct. For cats that have a food bowl waiting at home, dispensing with the hunt would certainly be no problem, but their cousins living in the wild could never afford to do that. And since the domestic cat has retained much of its wild heritage, it stalks mice with undaunted passion even if it hasn't caught anything for days. When playing with your cat, you can tell that the hunting instinct does not have to be aroused: Whether you let your pet "win" a hunting game or not, it always applies every one of its senses to the task.

251. Immobility reflex: **Why does a kitten stay still when its mother carries it by the scruff?**

To retrieve a kitten that has fallen out of the birthing box or to move her entire litter to a quieter spot, a mother cat grips her young by the scruff of the neck and carries it in her mouth. The little cat draws its hind legs and tail close to its body and automatically lapses into immobility. The reflex makes carrying easier and guards

In a safe hold: When being carried by its mother, a kitten goes limp.

against injury. The mother transports her young with her head held high, taking long steps.

252. In heat: **Why are some cats in heat fixated on a human being?**

A cat in heat attracts all the males in the neighborhood, but also tries to search for a suitable sex partner on her own (see Info, page 65). If that doesn't work, for lack of an alternative, cats that are alone in a household frequently select familiar humans or sometimes even canine friends as substitute partners and present themselves with all the attendant signs of readiness to mate. Petting the cat only causes these activities to intensify. Repeated stroking of her back can cause ovulation and result in pseudopregnancy.

253. Marking: **How do cats leave messages for their conspecifics?**

At prominent places in their territory and in their living environment as well, cats regularly leave visual and olfactory signs (marks) that provide other members of their species with important information: who left a card here and when, and probably even what mood the cat was in. Cats can even read messages that are several days old, but usually the marks are refreshed daily by the owners of the territory. Cats that pass through alien turf or wander along the boundaries of other territories also leave indications of their presence, preferably wherever they encounter the visual and scent signs of conspecifics. By rubbing its head, flanks, and rear end, the cat transfers its scents to certain objects, a procedure that it repeats several times during its territorial inspection tour. Toms also emit a powerful stream of urine, mixed with anal gland secretions, at strategically important points. The message, with its intense odor, is not missed, even by human noses. Female cats rarely mark in this way, and since it takes the form of a finely dispersed cloud of urine with no glandular secretions added, we are scarcely aware of it. Cats leave visual signs by sharpening their

CAT LANGUAGE

By their body language and vocalizations, cats make their moods and intentions unmistakably clear. In communicating with humans, too, cats employ many different language

FRIENDLY AND EVEN-TEMPERED
Body: head raised, coat smooth, tail motionless. Facial expression: ears pointed forward, pupils normal, whiskers at the side in resting position.

WIDE-AWAKE AND ALARMED
Body: taut, head extended, tail twitching. Facial expression: ears and whiskers in forward position, pupils enlarged.

TRYING TO IMPRESS
Body: in broadside position, legs stretched out, back and tail hair standing on end. Facial expression: ears laid back, pupils narrowed, eyes fixed on opponent.

UNCERTAIN AND FEARFUL
Body: pressed to the ground, legs bent (trying to look small), head averted, tail held close to body. Facial expression: ears pressed close, no visual contact. Voice: hissing to ward off opponent.

THREATENING AND READY TO ATTACK
Body: erect, tail held down, and head slightly to one side. Facial expression: eyes fixed on opponent, ears pointing back.

GREETING BEHAVIOR
Body: head raised, tail erect with tip bent. Facial expression: visual contact, whiskers outspread. Voice: meowing (with human), growling (with conspecifics).

techniques to lend emphasis to their demands. Every owner should be familiar with the most important feline vocabulary items.

MEOWING
Sound of kittens' mewing in distress. Rare in communication between adult cats. With humans: as a greeting and to get attention.

PURRING
Sound of well-being, but also used to win over or placate others. A sick cat purrs as a sign that it is ill and can't defend itself.

HISSING
Its mouth partly opened, the cat exhales quickly and sharply. Hissing is a sound of warning and threatening, intended to deter attackers and keep them at a distance.

SPITTING
Resembles hissing, but the breath is forced out even more rapidly and sometimes also through the nose. Produces a chilling effect, almost like a shot.

GROWLING
Low growling, like hissing and spitting, is used to warn and to threaten, for example, when another cat contests a cat's right to its food or prey.

BLEATING OR CHIRPING
Low sounds in rapid succession. Mouth slightly open, jaw chattering up and down. Typical sound when the cat sees prey that is out of reach.

claws on trees and other suitable spots. If claw grooming is the primary purpose, fallen tree trunks or branches will also be used, but for marking, a cat usually prefers vertical objects and places the message as high up on them as possible. In the process, the pads of the paws also dispense scents.

254. Mating: Why does a queen often react aggressively to a tom after mating?

By pressing her body to the ground, raising her rear end in the air, and laying her tail to one side, a female that is ready to mate invites the male to mount her. He mounts from behind, sinks his teeth into the back of her neck, and completes the act within a few seconds. While he is still joined to her, the queen cries out, turns toward him, hissing, and gives several powerful swats with her claws extended. This dismissive behavior is especially pronounced in inexperienced and nervous females. It is caused by the barbed penis, which painfully irritates the vagina as it withdraws. The barbs stimulate the vagina and trigger ovulation. The tom tries to break away from the queen as quickly as possible and get out of harm's way.

255. Mating: Why does a queen first keep turning down interested toms?

The queen's readiness to mate is governed by hormonal processes. Until she reaches that point, she will keep a male which is ready to mate at any time at a distance, but simultaneously make sure he stays interested in her. She repeatedly runs a few yard's away as soon as her suitor approaches, but then pauses, looks around at him, and makes sure he's still following her. Cat researcher Paul Leyhausen used the term "flirtation flight" for this behavior. Under some circumstances, such a "catch-me-if-you-can" game can go on for several days. With males that are familiar to her, the female often merely hints at the flirtation behavior or dispenses with it entirely.

256. Meowing: **Is meowing the most important sound in cat language?**

Kittens meow because they feel abandoned or cold. The complaining sound is an alarm signal for the mother, to which she reacts promptly. For adult cats, too, meowing retains this meaning, and they rarely make the noise among themselves. In communication with humans, however, this vocalization is at the top of the list: A cat meows when it needs a door opened, when it feels like cuddling and being petted, when it wants somebody to play with, when it is pointing out that a meal is overdue, or simply when it wants its human to pay more attention to it than to other things. These demands resemble the ones a kitten places on its mother. This is the role the cat sees itself playing: For it, the human is the mother cat or chief cat, who takes care of it and protects it just as its biological mother once did. In the partnership with a human, a cat does not become an adult; it stays a child and speaks to us in its children's language, of which meowing is a part.

257. Milk-treading or kneading: **When I pet my tom, he constantly flexes and extends his claws. What does this mean?**

Kittens stimulate their mother's milk flow by "treading," rhythmically kneading her teats and drawing the milk out. This behavior, known as milk-treading, is innate in cats. Adult animals lapse into treading whenever they feel especially contented: lying on the lap of a trusted human, being petted, or experiencing certain substances and fabrics (such as wool) as pleasant and "paw-friendly."

258. Petting: **My cat would even go without food in order to be petted. Why is this so important?**

Living in partnership with a human, a cat never grows up: The human is the chief cat, the cat remains the eternal child. And just as a kitten snuggles up to its feline mother, a pet cat needs our closeness and physical affection. A cat may become addicted to cuddling, especially if its owner has a sensitive touch and develops a feeling for which parts of the cat's body are especially receptive to petting. Petting and cuddling not only benefit the cat, but also have been proven to have a relaxing, calming effect on owners by stabilizing their heartbeats, steadying their breathing, lowering their blood pressure, and reducing their stress.

259. Petting: Why do some cats resist having their tummies rubbed?

Only when a cat completely trusts a human will it lie on its back or side and present its unprotected abdomen. It seeks eye contact and reinforces the invitation to petting by purring in a comforting way. Since the supine position is also assumed in self-defense, some cats are unable to suppress a protective pedaling of their hind legs, a reaction that appears distressing to the cat itself. Individual preferences vary widely, and there are cats that refuse to let their belly be touched at all.

260. Prey capture: Why do cats often delay their attack, although the mouse has been out of its hole for quite some time?

As a predator, the cat has a hard job. It takes a lot of time and effort to stalk quarry, crouching and under cover, as noiselessly as possible, and to get as close as possible. If the attack is too hasty, all the effort may be wasted. Often the hunter repeatedly prepares to spring (usually two to three shallow pounces), but pauses again. The deciding factor is whether the mouse has moved away from the entrance to its hole, so that it doesn't vanish from the scene at the last second. Further, domestic cats, like their wild relatives, prefer to attack from behind. In a frontal attack, there is always the risk that the prey will offer resistance and injure the hunter.

261. Purring: **Is purring always a sign that a cat feels fine?**

Cats use the purring sounds (see Info, page 203) produced in the larynx to signal that everything is all right. A mother cat purrs to calm her young. Adult cats purr when they feel at ease, but also to put others in a good mood. Even sick animals frequently purr, to convey in this way that they are weak and don't represent a threat to anyone.

262. Putting on an act: **Can cats lie?**

Like all higher mammals, cats too can dissemble in order to attain a certain goal. Generally this involves behavioral strategies that are dependent on appropriate positive feedback from the addressee. A cat is quick to register who its deceptive maneuvers succeed with. A good many cats procure benefits in this way, for example, in terms of sustenance: Though well fed, they produce heart-rending pleas and wails for certain family members to hear, and give the impression of being neglected and totally starving creatures in order to be spoiled with cat

> ### INFO
>
> **Behavior when ill**
> Many feline diseases result in a change in behavior often even before physical symptoms are discernible. Some examples are apathy in a cat with gastrointestinal problems, excessive licking with skin diseases, aggressiveness or avoidance of contact with infections, and refusal to eat with dental problems and gum inflammations.

treats. In comparison with animals that live in groups and herds, however, cats are less likely to employ bluffs and deceptive strategies.

263. Roaming: What triggers a cat's desire to roam?

Some cats have roaming in their blood, especially if their mother was always on the go. Toms have larger territories than queens, which are more inclined to be homebodies, and they explore strange territories more frequently and often disappear for several days. When it's time to mate, the urge to run away and roam is equally great in toms and queens. If a previously domesticated female becomes a roamer overnight, she usually doesn't feel happy at home anymore. There are many reasons: neglect, "jealousy" of a new family member (baby, dog, second cat), noise and chaos, a move. Sometimes, however, the prolonged absence also has a simple explanation, and the cat is letting the neighbors feed it and has found a cozy place to sleep somewhere. You can train your cat to stay closer to home by feeding it only after it comes back indoors and at fixed times, if at all possible. Spayed and neutered animals are less inclined to roam.

264. Rubbing its head: Why does a cat rub its head against other animals, humans, and objects?

Rubbing its head is a sign of affection toward animal and human friends and, like rubbing its flanks against them and putting its tail across its back, it is displayed primarily in greeting. By offering its head, the cat simultaneously transfers scents from skin glands on its chin, cheeks, and flanks and at the base of its tail, thus marking its personal property and familiar surroundings with its own particular fragrance. This includes furniture and other objects in its home and prominent objects (fences, posts, trees, shrubs, corners of buildings) in its territory. These scent marks are also a cat's way of leaving its calling card for all other conspecifics. Once a tom, and sometimes a queen, has deposited a scent mark with a well-aimed stream of urine, he then "coats" himself with his own scent again by rubbing his head against the place he has just marked. Then he rubs against other objects and thus transfers his smell once more.

265. Social behavior: **What does social behavior mean for a loner like the cat?**

Although all cats, except the lion, live as loners, they form a great many social bonds far more than scientists long believed possible. Lifelong friendships among housecats are not rare; some females raise their young jointly; toms join together in brotherhoods; and neighborhood cats repeatedly get together for a nighttime rendezvous. The great significance of social behavior for cats is also made clear by their highly developed and complex body language and vocalizations.

266. Success in mating: **Do big, strong toms have better chances as suitors?**

In the twinkling of an eye, the scent of a queen in heat summons every intact male in the entire neighborhood to the scene. Even sheltered indoor toms ignore the curfew during this time. At the queen's residence, therefore, the gentlemen almost always find competition; rarely is there only one suitor to be seen far and wide. With their loud singing, the toms try to impress each other, but they also get into serious scraps. The female usually sits on the fringe of these proceedings, apparently completely disinterested, and doesn't even watch the skirmish. After initially turning down her suitors, she finally encourages and accepts one of them. None of the males has anything to say about it; it is the female's decision alone. What the deciding factor for her is, is impossible to guess. Not infrequently she chooses a slight little fellow, and the big, husky fighters are left out in the cold.

267. Teat preference: Does each kitten really have its own special favorite teat?

A newborn kitten can neither see nor hear. It reacts only to warmth, touch, and scent and cries for help if it stops being aware of the nest smell or loses physical contact with its mother and littermates. Each kitten, after a short time, lays claim to its own teat, which it identifies by the smell and finds again and again. If another kitten wants to take over the favorite teat, it frequently is pushed away. The strongest kittens generally occupy the rear teats, which have the greatest milk flow.

268. Territorial behavior: Does a cat behave differently in its territory than elsewhere?

A cat inspects its territory at certain times of day and according to a fixed route plan, keeps a lookout from elevated vantage points (observation posts), leaves olfactory and visual marks, and checks out marks left by other cats. Strange cats are driven out of the territory and followed until they reach its border. Householder's rights bestow power: Interlopers usually come off second best even against physically inferior territory owners. The paths along the territory's boundaries generally are used by several cats. To avoid getting in each other's way, they adhere to a schedule that grants each cat the right of way at fixed times. From time to time, cats explore the strip of land bordering their territory, but here they assert no claims of ownership and avoid other cats as far as possible.

269. Thermal regulation: How does a cat keep from getting overheated?

The cat has only a few sweat glands and can't perspire all over. In high temperatures, it discharges heat by panting with its mouth open and wets its coat with its tongue to cool off through evaporation. Despite their thick coat, cats are amazingly heat-resistant and still feel comfortable when their skin temperature exceeds 92°F (50°C).

270. Threatening: When cats threaten each other, is it always intended seriously or sometimes just for show?

Threatening gestures have an important function in the animal kingdom because in many cases they prevent fights and potential injuries, even fatal ones. Cats have highly differentiated threat behavior, containing elements of body language and vocalization. When a cat is threatening to attack, the hair on its back and tail bristles (in a frightened cat, however, all the hair stands up), its tail points downward and is almost motionless, its eyes are fixed on the opponent, and its head is turned slightly to one side. Purely offensive threatening is rare; frequently various moods are superimposed in the threat. For example, the arching of the cat's back expresses a conflict between fear and readiness to attack. The threatening gestures are accompanied and reinforced by varying intensities of vocalizations, including specific facial expressions. Typical warning and threatening sounds are hissing, spitting, and growling, with the hissing being more a signal of defense, the growling more a signal of offense. Even kittens, in play-fighting, test the effect of threat gestures and try to impress their littermates by arching their back and bristling their hair.

INFO

Purring, a sound like no other
As a continuous tone, purring is close to setting a record: It's no problem for a cat to purr nonstop for several hours. The noises are produced in the larynx. Domestic cats can purr when inhaling and exhaling. It works even with a closed mouth, and kittens at their mother's teats don't even have to interrupt their nursing to purr. The individual spectrum is broad: Along with endurance purrers, there are also cats that refuse to purr.

271. Trying to impress: What does a cat want to achieve by seeking to impress other cats?

When trying to impress, a cat is demonstrating strength and self-confidence. In its own territory it thus makes it clear who's the boss. If another cat reveals that these gestures have the desired effect, that often spares the animals confrontations and injuries. In a typical impressive display, the cat presents itself broadside. Its legs are stretched, the hair on its back and tail bristles, its rear end is raised in the air, and its tail points at a downward angle. Arching its back is impressive but, at the same time, is an indication that fear and readiness to flee are present. When other cats are watching, claw sharpening is also used to impress, and the cat will scratch vigorously, sinking its claws high up on a tree trunk or a post. This behavior does not have to be learned: Kittens only a few weeks old know how to play the scene.

272. Vocalization: Cats are quiet animals. Is vocalization less important for them?

On the contrary, cats have an exceptionally large repertoire of vocalizations (see Cat Language, page 194), including at least sixteen basic sounds that are varied in many ways and have different meanings, independent of body language and facial expression. The meowing that we view as typical of cats plays a more secondary role in communication between adult cats. By cooing or purring (see Info, page 203), a cat expresses its feeling of well-being, while whimpering is usually a cry for help and a request for support (as when an abandoned kitten calls its mother), and hissing, spitting, and growling are unmistakable sounds of warning and threat-making. Further, there are a great many intermediate forms and variations that are typical of specific situations and actions, such as "chattering" or bleating and the chirping sounds with which a mother cat calls her young. By the age of 3 months, young cats know almost the entire vocabulary of feline language. Unlike humans, cats have no

> *Like humans, cats yawn when they're tired, but sometimes yawning is used to reassure and placate.*

need to rely on their sense of hearing to monitor the sounds they utter, so speech capability develops normally even in completely deaf animals. There are great differences in the degree of talkativeness, however, ranging from loud-voiced chatterboxes like the Siamese to the taciturn pussyfooters like the Persians and their relatives.

273. Warning cries: Is it true that cats have special warning cries for mice and rats?

While still in the birthing box, kittens learn the difference between a harmless mouse and a pugnacious rat. When the mother comes back from hunting with her prey, she summons her young with sounds that vary depending on the danger represented by the animal species she has caught. The "mouse cry" brings the kittens running without hesitation, but if their mother warns that she has a rat, they react cautiously and hesitantly. A cat also emits warning calls when it brings back only remnants of a prey animal.

274. Yawning: Why does my cat yawn sometimes, even when she isn't tired at all?

Like us, a cat yawns when it's sleepy, of course. But hearty yawning with a wide-open mouth has an additional significance in interspecies communication: It signals a cat's friendly mood and is meant to have a calming effect on other felines. In cat language, yawning means: I have no ill intentions and hope you're peacefully inclined as well. Especially between animals that are strangers, this usually prevents misunderstandings quickly and effectively.

275. Yowling tomcat: **Are male cats serenading a female when they yowl?**

The tom's vocal interludes, usually rather unmelodious, are not meant for the female in heat, but only for his rivals in seeking the lady's favor: The songs are the battle cries of the assembled suitors. The queen seems especially impressed neither by the vocal skills nor by the combat effectiveness of the gentleman callers. She alone makes the choice, and often enough she decides on a rather unprepossessing, quiet little male and ignores the Rambos and squallers. Sometimes the lovesick males are amazingly peaceful, however, or even dispense completely with a test of strength. This can be seen especially in residential areas with a large cat population and small, overlapping territories that can't be defended on a 24-hour basis. If a tom keeps starting trouble with his neighbors here, he'll quickly burn himself out.

Training, Playing, and Keeping Active

Cats are inquisitive and always up for a game. Here you will learn ways to motivate your pet to get involved with easy, fun-filled training techniques, solutions that prevent boredom, and methods of testing your cat's intelligence.

276. Baby and cat: I'm expecting a baby. Will our cat accept it?

At first a cat is mistrustful of every change in the family. Especially pronounced is its distant attitude toward new family members (both humans and animals) because it fears that its rights and claims are threatened. In particular, indoor cats that have built a close relationship with their owner will frequently be extremely stand-offish. The reactions of a "jealous" cat range from apathy, refusal to eat, and indoor soiling to aggressive behavior and an increased tendency to roam. Here's how to prevent jealous scenes: As soon as the baby has arrived, let the cat get acquainted with it and sniff it, in your presence. In the first few weeks, show a lot of attention to your cat whenever the newborn is in the room, but pay less notice to it at other times. The intended message will quickly be understood: If the baby is near, I do really well! But even if a cat cottons up to the new addition to the family, don't leave it unattended in the baby's room.

277. Begging: How do I break my tom of his habit of begging?

It always takes two for begging to occur, and it's hardly surprising that a kitty gets a taste for it if he's fed at the table or gets a treat every time he starts his wails of "Poor hungry cat." With some cats,

"Lead me not into temptation" is the best prescription for putting a stop to begging and snitching food.

Sometimes a cardboard box is the right place to get cozy and hide. And you can chew on it too.

this begging behavior has developed such momentum of its own that the food has become secondary, and they even eat sweets and things containing alcohol, which does not appeal to the feline palate and also is unhealthy. The therapy is simple, but demands some backbone and persistence on the owner's part. Serve food only in the bowl, make here-a-bite-and-there-a-bite part of the past, and offer a treat as a reward only in exceptional cases. Your cat will lack appreciation for this and make an uproar. At least in the first few weeks, it should be banished from the room when you sit down to eat. That will prevent the risk of your possibly giving in to its begging.

278. Being alone: Until now we've scarcely left our 8-month-old kitten by itself. How do we get it accustomed to being alone?

When a cat is tired and wants to nap, it's grateful to be left undisturbed. Consequently, start training it to be alone right after playtime or mealtime. At first, leave your kitten alone only briefly, and gradually lengthen the times if there are no protests. Don't lock the cat in just one room, and make sure the litter box, scratching post, and water bowl are accessible. If you plan to be away from home for a longer period, a handful of kibble will keep your pet from getting too hungry. Give the kitten toys that it can use only during your absence, and reserve a window seat with a view for it. Before leaving, check to make sure the household is safe for the kitten (see Household Dangers, page 54).

279. Biting: Should I let it pass when my kitten uses its teeth while we're playing?

Under no circumstances! Cats have an innate bite inhibition. It ensures that no injuries are inflicted during playful tussling or when the male grips the female's nape during mating. When hunting, then, a cat first has to learn to suppress its bite inhibition. A kitten still in the whelping box, however, has no idea how hard it can bite when playing, but its littermates teach it quickly and protest with loud squeals if the sharp little teeth ever nip too fiercely. By the time they go to their new homes, most kittens have learned the lesson, but sometimes they forget in the heat of the game that a human's skin is easier to injure than the coat of other cats. Stop the game if your kitten bites or scratches, and let it know from your wails that the attack was painful. Give it a toy that it can use to release excess energy (such as a fishing rod with a dangling toy). Don't engage in play-fighting with little ruffians that refuse to learn. Biting and swatting, however, can also be warning signals when the cat loses interest in the game.

280. Boredom: My cat turns the house upside down on a regular basis. What can I do?

A cat usually gets into mischief when it doesn't have enough to keep it busy. This applies mainly to cats that are left alone for hours and aren't allowed to go outdoors. Cats adapt their daily routine to that of their owners and use the time alone for a lengthy nap. In a prolonged absence, however, the naptimes alternate with active phases in which the cat wants to get the exercise it needs. For lack of alternatives, it climbs the curtains, digs in the flowerpot, and sharpens its claws on doors, rugs, and cushions. Cat-appropriate games and activity alternatives offer a remedy: an attractive scratch tree, a roll-a-snack ball, a rustling play sack, a play tunnel, a scented toy, a cat ladder and climbing rope, cat grass, cardboard boxes with peepholes for hiding in and chewing on, and of course the obligatory toy mouse. Remove the occasion for sin until the cat has learned to behave: Cover the flower-pots with plastic protectors (found in specialty stores), tie up the curtains (especially with young cats), and put the plants away if they keep getting gnawed on or mis-used as climbing trees. Play with your cat before you leave the house: If it's tired, it will do less mischief. If the cat is alone on a regular basis, it

For the cat to accept the scratching post, it must be placed where the cat often lingers.

needs a second cat as a partner, to avoid becoming emotionally stunted.

281. Children and cats: How do children keep from getting hurt when playing with the cat?

Explain to your children the way a cat behaves and the warning signals it uses to indicate that it doesn't want to play anymore. Children should heed these rules when dealing with cats:

➤ Never pull its tail, legs, or ears, and never stick your hand in the cat's face.
➤ Avoid loud yelling and wild arm-waving.
➤ Don't pet the cat's coat the wrong way.
➤ Don't cover the cat with a pillow, wrap it up in a blanket, or make it wear a "costume."
➤ Don't run after it shouting, and don't throw toys at it.
➤ Picking up the cat is taboo for younger children. Both child and cat can get hurt.
➤ When playing at close range, keep your face out of reach of paws and claws. If at all possible, wear long-sleeved clothing.

➤ Never ask the cat to play when it is sleeping or eating.

282. Claw sharpening: How can I get our cat to sharpen its claws on the scratching post?

No indoor kitty is interested in a scratching post off in a dark corner. The best location is a place halfway between its bed and its food bowl because the cat uses this route several times a day. Resting places and sleeping boxes at different heights, climbing ropes, and fishing-rod toys increase the scratching post's appeal. In addition, rub the trunk and scratching areas with catnip or valerian. By making scratching motions, show your cat where it can sharpen its claws. Cover the unwanted scratching places in your home with plastic wrap until the scratch tree has found 100% acceptance.

283. Detaching from the mother cat: Do you need to teach a kitten to become independent?

Starting in the sixth week, a young cat gradually becomes independent, but until it goes to a new home at 12 weeks, its mother continues to ensure that it learns all the lessons that matter in a cat's life. Then, the earlier the kitten comes to trust its new family, the

EXTRA TIP

Answering to its name

Suitable names for a cat are one- or two-syllable words with open vowels: The tried-and-true Fluffy or Mini are fine, but Sally, Maxi, Lilli, and a thousand others are just as good. The tone of voice makes the music: Call your cat in a soft, gentle voice, so that it always links the name with pleasant things. If your pet has misbehaved and is being reprimanded, never use its name to rebuke it. Even the best-behaved cat, however, is not as obedient as a dog.

more self-confident and outgoing it will be. That requires devotion, as well as regular activity to satisfy its curiosity and urge to explore. The cat's receptivity to learning is especially pronounced at this time. With loving guidance, it will grasp quickly what is allowed and what is taboo, and it will pay heed to these experiences the rest of its life.

284. Food envy: How do I keep my cats from challenging each other over food?

When one cat eats everything in the other's bowl, it rarely has anything to do with hunger. Dominant animals demonstrate their claim to power in this way, and some feline foodies are obviously convinced that the tastier menu is in the other bowl. Therapy: Fill the food bowl with food that the cat doesn't like, or trickle some lemon juice on top. The food thief usually will be converted after the very first taste. Repeat offenders must be fed in separate rooms or at different times.

285. Intelligence: Can you test to see how smart a cat is?

You can get your cat into brain training with brain-teasers at varying levels of difficulty, and usually it will have fun in the process.

➤ Brain test for beginners: Put a favorite toy or a treat in a box. Cover it with something that is easily removable. Let the cat watch while you hide it. Some will find it on the first try, while others need several warm-ups.

➤ For advanced cats: Put an object in a box, as above. Before encouraging the cat to find it, distract your pet for a short time.

➤ For experts: Put the object in one of three boxes. Begin by playing with the boxes open, and cover the object after the cat has successfully found it several times.

➤ For pros: Use three boxes, as above. After hiding the object, switch the boxes in the cat's presence.

The tests are even harder with glass containers than cardboard boxes: The cat sees the object and tries to grab the glass with its paw.

286. Jealousy: Our cat is a sensitive creature, jealous of everyone. What causes this?

Cats watch like hawks to ensure that their interests and privileges are not diminished. It is a biologically useful behavior, which ensures the survival of our domestic cat's relatives living in the wild but remains equally pronounced in the housecat as well. In its territory, that works relatively easily: unwanted intruders are driven away. But the owner's new life partner, baby, second cat, or new dog can't be gotten rid of the same way. The closer the cat's bond with its special human, the more vehement is its reaction when it feels set back or neglected. Cats are excellent observers in this regard and immediately take note if, for example, the animal competitor in the household is shown preference. Toms generally are more tolerant, but jealousy can become a real problem for female cats. Make sure the cat can withdraw to its private zone at all times without being disturbed by a new pet. Don't overtly show affection to the new addition when the cat is present. Don't throw your pet's daily routine into confusion; adhere to the usual mealtimes and times for playing and cuddling. Ask your new life partner to take over the feeding and care of the cat.

EXTRA TIP

One-on-one teaching
Cats are curious and interested in everything. With training exercises, that's not necessarily an advantage. To keep your pupil from being distracted, always hold the lesson in the same place. Playmates and observers, humans and cats must stay outside. One-on-one instruction is especially important with young cats, which quickly forget everything else when something new is going on.

287. Leash: **Will every cat accept a leash and collar?**

Kittenhood is virtually the only time cats can be successfully taught to wear a leash; most adult cats resist with all their might when you want to put a collar on them. Exceptions are especially acquiescent breeds such as Persians and Maine Coons as well as, surprisingly, many Siamese. More suitable than the collar is a chest harness, which the cat can't slip out of. Even if your cat accepts the leash, it will never react as obediently to it as a dog. You need to schedule plenty of time and patience for your walks, and even then you won't get much farther than around the block.

288. Mice: **My cat keeps dragging mice into the house. How can I break him of the habit?**

The mother cat brings home mice and other rodents from her hunting expedition first dead ones, and then live prey. From her, the young learn how to deal with prey animals. Though a cat regards its human owner as chief cat, it obviously considers him or her incapable of going out hunting. Consequently, the cat takes on the responsibility of providing sustenance and more or less regularly brings prey home, which it usually also announces quite loudly. Offer your pet a treat in exchange and dispose of the "love gift" as discreetly as possible. Quite a few cat owners are convinced that their darling will lose the craving to hunt if it is plentifully fed, but the cat's hunting instinct does not depend on the degree of its satiety. Ultimately, well-fed cats even have greater success as hunters because they are especially capable and fit, and they "delight" their human more often with a little mouse than other cats.

289. Neighbors: **What do I do if there's trouble with the neighbors over the cat?**

For a free-roaming cat, fences and walls are no obstacle, and it considers the properties in the neighborhood as being part of its home territory too. Then it's a recipe for disaster if the cat defecates on the neighbor's well-manicured lawn, goes fishing in the garden pond, or digs in the flower and vegetable beds. Current jurisprudence allows the keeping of a cat with outdoor privileges, in rural areas, even two cats. If at all possible, don't let the dispute get all the way to the courts. Whatever the judge's decision, neighborly relations are usually permanently impaired afterward. To put a stop to undesirable actions on a neighbor's property, you have to catch the cat red-handed and spray it with a water pistol, for example. More practical and likelier to succeed are alternative opportunities in your own yard: several places to hide and rest, a digging area with fresh soil, special perches, and perhaps also an additional litter box, sheltered from wind and the elements. Metal guard collars around the trees protect birds' nests.

290. Party pooper: What toy can I use to entice a party pooper to join in?

The more of its senses a toy appeals to, the more interesting it is for a cat. Scarcely any cat is left cold when offered balls that click or rustle, smell bewitchingly of catnip, or even release little treats (roll-a-snack balls). A valerian-scented toy mouse is just as irresistible as a crunch tunnel or the mysterious rustling play sack, which are lined with a crackling material. And even hardcore spoilsports for whom a normal ball is too boring will feel an itch in their paws once they see the wild leaps of a zigzag ball.

291. Peace at night: My cat wants to go outside every night. How can I teach him to keep civilized hours?

Play with your tom regularly in the evenings and postpone his feeding to just before bedtime. Then he probably will be so tired that a nap seems far more desirable to him than his nightly stalk. Alternative: If you treat your cat to his own cat door, he can come and go without disturbing you.

292. Pet toilet training: What do I do if the kitten isn't toilet-trained?

➤ Play it safe: In the first few days after the kitten's arrival, place it in the litter box after every meal.
➤ Show how it's done: Using your hand, scratch in the litter to get the kitten to emulate you.
➤ Choose a good place: Sometimes there's a lot of pressure on the bladder. Then a little kitten has to be able to get to the litter box in a hurry.
➤ Experiment with litter: Especially sensitive young animals sometimes have problems with an unfamiliar type of litter. Try several kinds.

293. Playing: Are there different types of play preferences among cats?

When playing, cats develop individual preferences. Test to see what especially inspires your pet: climbing and jumping, hunting and catching prey, hide-and-seek, brain-teasers and guessing games, tussling or cuddling games. Ball games, which almost all cats enjoy, are classics. Top athletes like Somalis and Siamese need athletic challenge, while the Chartreux and the Persian like quieter games.

294. Punishment: Is it all right to punish the cat if it has misbehaved?

Naturally, you don't yell at a cat or go so far as to hit it. A vigorous, long-drawn-out "Nooooo!" is permissible, however. But you should use it only when you catch your cat red-handed; otherwise, your pet can't associate the misbehavior with the criticism. Also effective is a light tap on the nose or a gentle puff of breath. The whiff of air on its face will be understood by every cat as a warning signal because it also occurs when cats, hissing and spitting, give each other a piece of their mind and expel air in explosive bursts. The rebuke should be a rare exception, used only for serious misdeeds. Instead, solve problems by offering your cat attractive alternatives that make the problem behavior uninteresting.

295. Retrieving: My sister's cat can retrieve like a dog. Can I teach my tomcat to do this?

?

Almost every cat will chase after a ball or a crumpled piece of paper. Bringing it back is another matter, however. Some cats are passionate retrievers, while others wouldn't even dream of it. Here's how to encourage your tom's interest in retrieving: Offer him a second toy as soon as he has gotten hold of the first object, ideally a really tempting squeaky animal or a rattle. Position yourself strategically so that he has to run toward you if he wants to remove the toy to a safe place. Cats frequently will head for their beds. Of course, you'll want to shower your tom with praise and pet him if he actually drops the old toy in front of you and accepts the new one. A treat is also a good replacement object, but don't overdo it and let your pet's figure suffer. Repeat the exercise daily. Even if your tom participates enthusiastically, don't expect him to retrieve the way a dog does.

INFO

Invitation to play

When a cat is in the mood to play, it encourages a human in typical fashion to show a follow-up reaction, galloping around with its body turned broadside, with legs stiffened and tail raised high. "Try to catch me!" is the unmistakable message. If the human fails to respond to the invitation, the action usually is repeated several times. Originally this behavior is part of mating foreplay, during which the female keeps running away from her suitor.

296. Rewards: **Our dachshund will do anything for a treat. Can cats also be motivated with rewards?**

Cats are considered trainable only to a limited extent and unwilling to learn. That is true only if you use training methods that get results with a dog. With a dog, the motivation is clear: It wants to fulfill every wish of its pack leader and does everything to garner praise and recognition. A cat's behavior is more egotistical; it is cooperative only if it's in the mood or sees some advantage in the action. It is easiest to get a cat's participation by appealing to its enjoyment of exercise and its hunting instinct. Treats offered as rewards usually fail to have the desired effect: A hungry cat is totally focused on the food and forgets everything else, while a full cat can't be tempted even with the tastiest delicacy.

297. Stealing: **Can you put a stop to a cat's stealing?**

The safest way to stop a cat from snitching food is not to lead it into temptation: If your pet is alone, everything edible must be out of reach. Hunger plays almost no role; almost always it is curiosity and the smell of food that leads a cat to forbidden activities, especially if it believes it is unobserved. If you catch it red-handed, a squirt from the water pistol is permissible. With many transgressors, the can trick works: Tie a cord to an empty tin can, put the can at the edge of the table, and conceal some delicious-smelling bits of meat under it. If the cat tugs at the cord, the can falls to the floor with a loud clatter. The shock therapy can be beneficial. The originator of the campaign must remain out of sight; otherwise, the cat will hold him or her responsible for the scare.

298. Toys: What are the hallmarks of good, safe cat toys?

Here's what to look for when buying cat toys:

➤ The toy is made of heavy-duty material that can't be bitten into (hard plastic, wood, hide, sisal).

➤ The metal center (squeaker) inside squeaky toys must be solidly coated.

➤ There are no protruding metal, plastic, or glass parts that can injure the cat.

➤ Wooden toys must not splinter; make sure the edges are rounded.

➤ Balls should not be swallowed and must be at least the size of a ping-pong ball. Golf and squash balls are suitable.

➤ Free of poisonous dyes and coatings.

➤ Balls of yarn are not suitable cat toys because cats can get entangled or can swallow them.

➤ Objects for chewing must be harmless, such as corrugated cardboard from packing crates.

299. Training: Can cats be trained at all?

You won't achieve anything through prohibitions, withdrawal of affection, or standardized training sessions. A cat has to be tempted to participate and to learn.

➤ Arousing curiosity: Ideally, use toys that appeal to as many of the senses as possible (scented objects, rattles, balls that click) and games of hide-and-seek.

➤ Inspiring imitation: Cats have marvelous powers of observation. These super-clever creatures get the hang of something after seeing it once provided they're having a good time. Start with simple, short exercises.

➤ Setting school hours: Always practice with your cat at a certain time of day and never for longer than 15 minutes. It must be wide-awake and in a good temper. No lessons after meals.

➤ Establishing classroom rules: Train with your cat in familiar surroundings and repeat every lesson several times. Stop the class if your pet loses interest, is distracted, or gets tired.

Long-running hit: The sphere that rolls in a circle when nudged by a paw fascinates many cats over and over again.

➤ Using teaching aids: Reserve certain playthings exclusively for the lessons, to keep them from losing their charm over time.

➤ Employing proper form of address: Call your cat by its name (see Tip, page 214) in a soft, gentle voice in order to get its attention.

300. Traveling: Our cat fights tooth and claw against its pet carrier. What can keep it from being afraid?

If the cat associates its travel accommodations with unpleasant experiences (car rides, vet), it needs patience and understanding until it overcomes its fear. Put the carrier in a favorite resting place of the cat's, one that is elevated, if possible, and put its favorite blanket inside. Leave the mesh door open, with the interior exuding a tempting scent of catnip toy and, from time to time, a treat. Pet and praise your cat if it goes inside voluntarily. After about 2 or 3 weeks, it should have accepted the pet carrier as part of its private property.

THE BEST CAT TOYS

All cats are enthusiastic about classic toys like toy mice, feather toys, and rubber balls. But play tunnels, rustling play sacks, catnip pillows, and fun lights can also make things lively.

BALLS
Solid rubber balls, zigzag balls, cage balls, soft balls, and many more are just right for retrieving, for "soccer games," and for boisterous games of chase.

MICE
Bite-resistant furry mice, sisal mice, and squeaky mice (also with original mouse sound) make even tired cats frisky.

TEASER TOYS
A bungee mouse, feather tassels, and a toy fishing rod with a rubber band will train your pet to jump and improve its reaction time.

PLAY TUNNEL
The play tunnel invites a cat to hide and explore, especially if it is lined with crinkly, rustling material.

SCENTED TOYS
Mint pillows and catnip mice get cats addicted (guaranteed: no adverse reactions). Not every cat reacts to the scents, however.

FUN LIGHT
When chasing the dancing dots of light produced by the fun light and magic mouse, cats can forget the whole world.

Glossary of Terms from A to Z

➤ Ability to find the way home
Cats use optical marks and auditory images with familiar and pronounced sounds to orient themselves.

➤ Anal display
The mutual sniffing of the anal region is part of the feline *greeting ritual*. The anal glands at the sides of the anus generate a distinctive scent.

➤ Ancestry
The domestic cat is descended from the African wild cat. The first ancestor is thought to have been the Nubian kaffir cat, *Felis sylvestris lybica*, native to Egypt and the area north of the Sahara, which is very similar to the house cat in behavior and appearance.

➤ Arched back
Part of a cat's system of body language, in which a threat to attack and a desire to flee (fight or flight response) are present simultaneously.

➤ Bezoars
When grooming its coat, a cat swallows hairs, which can form bezoars (hairballs) in the stomach. Most bezoars are regurgitated, which is easier for the cat to do if it nibbles on cat grass and green plants.

➤ Big cats
The big cats include the lion, leopard, tiger, jaguar, and snow leopard. Unlike the *small cats*, they can roar, but they purr only when exhaling.

➤ Bite inhibition
The bite inhibition ensures that no injuries are suffered in play-fighting. When hunting, the cat must overcome its innate bite inhibition.

➤ Body language
Body language is an important form of expression in *cat language*.

➤ Breed registry
It is maintained by the breed club and lists all the litters of a pedigreed cat. The *pedigree* is an excerpt from the breed registry (stud book).

➤ Breed standard
The standard describes the ideal characteristics of a breed. It is issued by the breed association and is the basis for judging cats at shows.

➤ Carnassial teeth
The carnassial teeth are typical of a *predator*; they include

the last premolar in the upper jaw and the molar in the lower jaw. The cat uses them to cut pieces of meat from the prey.

➤ **Cat allergy**
Allergic reaction by many people to the saliva that the cat distributes throughout its coat when washing. Symptoms: watery eyes, sneezing, breathing difficulties.

➤ **Cat language**
To communicate, cats use *body language, facial expressions,* and vocalizations, in addition to visual signs and scent marks.

➤ **Clavicle**
Owing to the greatly reduced clavicles, the cat's rib cage is narrow, which enables it to slip through very narrow gaps.

➤ **Claw sharpening**
In the sharpening process, old protective outer layers are removed and the newly grown claws are sharpened. Also used for purposes of *marking* and *trying to impress.*

➤ **Color vision**
The cat's eye can tell colors apart, but it has little receptivity for red. In the feline world, movements play a far more important role than colors.

➤ **Colostrum**
Also: foremilk. Secreted by mother after giving birth, it is especially rich in antibodies and protects the young against infections in the first few weeks.

➤ **Comfort behavior**
Behaviors designed to promote personal hygiene and a sense of well-being.

➤ **Dance of relief**
After a successful hunt, a cat dances around its prey, leaping high in the air, to relieve tension and agitation.

➤ **Displacement behavior**
Behavior that is not appropriate to the situation and is displayed usually when a decision is hard to make. Typically, a cat washes its coat as a form of displacement when it doesn't know whether to attack an enemy or run away.

➤ **Domestication**
By artificial selection, humans have made wild animals useful. With the exception of the cat, all other such creatures are herd and pack animals, like the dog, sheep, goat, cow, pig, and horse.

➤ **Dominance**
In *genetics*: dominant genes suppress the expression of recessive traits (*recessiveness*). In behavioral research: a

dominant animal takes on a leadership role.

➤ **Facial expressions**
The expressions on a cat's face reveal its mood and are used for communication (*cat language*).

➤ **Felidae**
Scientific name for the cat family, distributed worldwide. The Felidae include the *big cats* and the *small cats*. The cheetah has a special position.

➤ **Flehmen response**
A flehming cat is examining scents with its *Jacobson's organ*. The flehmen response is triggered by strong olfactory stimuli, in a tom, for example, by the smell of a queen in heat.

➤ **Fondness for gaps**
Term from behavioral science for the pronounced fondness cats develop for caves, gaps, and hiding places.

➤ **Genes**
The genes are located on the chromosomes in the cell nucleus. As carriers of inherited material, they are responsible for the expression of characteristics.

➤ **Genetics**
Genetics (the study of heredity) deals with the mechanisms that govern the transmission of characteristics.

➤ **Gestation period**
Kittens are born after 63 days. The young of some purebred cats are born after only 58–60 days.

➤ **Greeting ritual**
When cats meet, they make nose-to-nose contact. Smell plays the leading role here, but the whiskers and tactile hairs also supply important information. The nose check follows the examination of the *anal display*.

➤ **Hearing ability**
Cats react especially to high tones and can perceive even sounds in the ultrasonic range up to 70,000 Hz (humans: 20,000 Hz).

➤ **Heat (Estrus)**
A queen goes into heat when eggs capable of being fertilized form in her ovaries. She is restless, meows and calls, rolls on the ground, and is now ready to conceive. If she is not serviced, the heat cycle recurs several times in spring and fall.

➤ **Hierarchy**
Hierarchy is less obvious among cats than among dogs. Rank is often expressed by optical and olfactory signals (*marking*).

> **Hunting by stealth**

Except for the cheetah, which runs down its prey, all cats use the stalk-and-pounce method of hunting prey.

> **Immobility reflex**

When a kitten is carried by its mother, the reflex causes its body to become immobile.

> **Incubation period**

The time between infection and the development of symptoms, depending on the disease, from a few hours or days (cat flu) to several years (leukemia).

> **Infectious diseases**

Most feline infectious diseases are viral in origin. Immunity to the most dangerous diseases is provided only by vaccination. Inoculations can be given to prevent rabies, cat flu, feline distemper (FP), leukemia (FeLV), and FIP. There is also a vaccine against FIV (cat AIDS) which has not yet been approved globally.

> **Internal clock**

An internal (biological) clock obviously exists in plants and animals as well as in humans. It controls metabolic processes and behavior in a roughly 24-hour cycle.

> **Jacobson's organ**

Also: vomeronasal organ. Olfactory organ in the nasal mucosa that opens into the roof of the mouth. It also allows cats to detect sex hormones (*Flehmen response*).

> **Key stimulus**

Stimulus that sets certain behaviors in motion. Rustling, crinkling, and the squeaking of a mouse are acoustic key stimuli that trigger the prey-capturing behavior of a cat. A visual key stimulus is the movement of small animals when they flee.

> **Legal liability**

Pet owners are legally liable for damage caused by their pet. Cats are included in the coverage provided by personal liability insurance.

> **Longhaired cats**

Longhaired cats have been in existence for several centuries. They probably originated through spontaneous mutation. Persians, with guard hair 5 to 6 inches (12 to 15 cm) in length, have the longest coat.

> **Marking**

By rubbing its head and flanks against animals, humans, and objects, a cat marks them with scents. Scent is also transferred during *claw sharpening*.

> **Mating position**

The queen ducks, raises her rear end, and holds her tail to one side. The male mounts her from behind and sinks his teeth into her nape. Copulation itself lasts only a few seconds.

➤ Microchip
The veterinarian implants the microchip (transponder) under the cat's skin. The animal's identification number can be read by a special scanning device.

➤ Milk-treading
Nursing kittens rhythmically knead their mother's teats with their paws to stimulate her milk flow. Adult cats also make the kneading movements when they feel contented.

➤ Neutering
Surgical removal of a female cat's ovaries (sometimes also of the uterus) or of a male cat's testicles. A neutered cat is infertile.

➤ Nictitating membrane
Third eyelid, usually concealed in the inner corner of the eye, used partly to keep the eyeball moist. Frequently visible when a cat is ill.

➤ Odd-eyed
Iris heterochromy: cat with different-colored eyes, one blue and one often brownish or copper-colored.

➤ Pacini corpuscles
Pressure sensors in the balls of the paws that react to the tiniest vibrations.

➤ Pedigree
Excerpt from the *breed registry* or stud book of the breed club. The pedigree (or family tree) is the list of the ancestors of a purebred cat. The registry gives the breed, sex, color, date of birth, registration number, cattery name, and individual name, as well as the lineage.

➤ Place memory
Cats memorize the details of their familiar surroundings (home environment and territory) and register even the tiniest changes.

➤ Points
Coat coloration with a pale body and darker extremities. Typical of Siamese and Balinese.

➤ Predator's teeth
Typical of a predator's dentition are the long, curved incisors and canines known as *carnassial teeth*.

➤ Prey-catching behavior
The cat's prey-catching behavior is triggered by high-frequency sounds (scurrying, rustling, whispering of mice) and by small, rapidly moving objects.

➤ Pseudopregnancy
Hormonal changes can cause a cat that has not been cov-

ered to behave like a pregnant queen after heat has ended. The teats become swollen, and often even lactation occurs.

➤ **Pupillary reflex**
Adaptation of pupil size to light intensity: in bright light, narrowed to a slit; in low light, enlarged. Pupil size also expresses a cat's mood.

➤ **Purebred cats**
A breed is recognized by certain characteristics (coat, frame, character) that are common to all animals of the breed and are passed on to the offspring.

➤ **Purring**
By the purring of her young, a mother cat knows that everything is all right. Adult cats use purring to convey their feeling of well-being and also to placate. Sick cats purr to indicate that they are helpless and weak. The purring sounds are produced in the larynx. Like all other *small cats*, the house cat can purr when exhaling and inhaling.

➤ **Recessiveness**
In genetics, an allele is termed recessive if it is suppressed by other alleles. In cats, for example, being longhaired is a recessive trait.

➤ **Registration**
Registration in a pet register (such as that maintained by the German Animal Welfare League) increases the chance of finding missing animals again.

➤ **REM phase**
Sleep phase recognizable by rapid eye movements beneath the closed lids. Also typical of REM sleep is the flaccidity of the muscles. The cat dreams during the REM phase.

➤ **Semi-longhaired cats**
Pedigreed cats whose guard hair is shorter and whose undercoat is less dense than those of *longhaired cats*. Typical of Maine Coons and Norwegian Forest Cats.

➤ **Sense of equilibrium**
The balance (vestibular) system of the ear reports deviations from the normal position to the cerebellum, which controls movement. Cats have a well-developed sense of balance.

➤ **Sexing**
Female: The slit-shaped vaginal opening is right beneath the anus. Male: Between the anus and the rounded sexual opening are the testicles, visible in a young tom only as a faint bulge.

➤ **Sex-linked heredity**
The genetic material (*genes*) of the sex chromosomes is inherited in a sex-linked manner. As a consequence of such a heredity, three-colored cats (*tortoise-shell*) are always female.

➤ **Shorthaired cats**
The ancestors of the domestic cat were shorthaired, and today too, most cats have a short coat. Genetically, short hair is dominant.

➤ **Sleep phases**
In sleep, non-REM phases and REM phases alternate. Non-REM sleep is divided into light and deep stages. In light sleep, a cat reacts to every strange noise.

➤ **Small cats**
Small cats are unable to roar like the *big cats*, but they can purr when exhaling and inhaling. In addition to wild cats (with *Felis sylvestris lybica* as the ancestor of the house cat), they include the lynx, serval, ocelot, and puma.

➤ **Stereoscopic vision**
The cat's fields of view overlap in a sector of 130 degrees, in which the animal sees stereoscopically. Spatial vision

is a precondition for measuring distance.

➤ **Stereotypes**
Uniform, usually frequently repeated behaviors. Stereotyped behaviors are especially common in zoo animals and caged animals. In cats, they can be triggered by stress and lack of activity and may result in self-mutilation and disease.

➤ **Sterilization**
Surgical procedure intended to end fertility in male and female cats. Since only the fallopian tubes or spermatic cords are severed, the sex drive is preserved, in contrast to the process of *neutering*.

➤ **Tapetum lucidum**
Light-reflecting layer (usually made up of guanine crystals) at the back of the eye in many vertebrates. The reflection increases the light yield and thus improves vision in dim light. The cat's eyes glow when light shines on them from the front.

➤ **Tattooing**
Identification with a number (combination of numerals and letters) in the ear.

➤ **Teat preference**
Newborn kittens usually seek their own "personal" teat, which they recognize by its smell. The hindmost and most productive teats are

claimed by the strongest kittens.

➤ Teething
Between the third and seventh (or eighth) months, the thirty permanent teeth replace the kitten's twenty-six milk teeth.

➤ Territory
The house cat's territory usually directly adjoins the place where it lives, the primary home. On its stalking rounds, the owner of the territory monitors the terrain and emphasizes its claim to ownership with visual and olfactory marks (*marking*). Strange cats are attacked and driven out. The size of the territory depends on the topographical features and the density of the feline population. Outside of the territory is the border area, which is also used by other cats.

➤ Thermal regulation
Maintenance of body temperature. The capacity for thermal regulation is not yet fully developed in kittens during the first 6 weeks of life.

➤ Tortoise-shell
Coat with markings in three colors (brown, black, yellowish). Tortoise-shell cats are almost always female; tortoise-shell males are sterile.

➤ Toxoplasmosis
Infectious disease that is also communicable to humans (*zoonoses*) but usually produces no symptoms. It is a threat to pregnant women.

➤ Trying to impress
A cat that is trying to impress demonstrates strength in order to intimidate an opponent, for example by an *arched back* or by *claw sharpening*.

➤ Vibrissae
Tactile hairs on the cat's face, including the whiskers and the individual hairs on the chin and cheeks and above the eyes. Vibrissae react to every tactile stimulus.

➤ Walking on tiptoes
When they walk, cats put only the tips of their finger and toe bones on the ground. The cushions on their soles enable them to move without making a sound.

➤ Zoonoses
Diseases that are communicable by animals to humans and vice versa. In the case of cats, we can become infected, for example, with rabies, salmonellosis, ringworm, and *toxoplasmosis*.

Index

Useful Addresses and Literature

Associations and Clubs

American Association of Cat Enthusiasts (AACE)
P.O. Box 213
Pine Brook, NJ 07058
(973)335-6717
www.aaceinc.org

American Cat Association (ACA)
8101 Katherine Avenue
Panorama City, CA 91402
(818)781-5656

American Cat Fanciers Association (ACFA)
P.O. Box 1949
Nixa, Mo 65714-1949
(417)725-1530
www.acfacat.com

American Society for the Prevention of Cruelty to Animals (ASPCA)
424 East 92nd Street
New York, NY 10128
(212)876-7700
www.aspca.org

Animal Poison Control Center
(888)426-4435

Internet Addresses

www.cats.about.com
www.petinsurance.com

For questions about the care of cats, contact your local pet store dealer, animal shelter, or veterinarian.

Books

Carlson, Delbert G., D.V.M., and Giffin, James M., M.D. *Cat Owner's Veterinary Handbook.* Howell Book House, New York, 1983

Davis, Karen Leigh. *The Cat Handbook.* Barron's Educational Series, Inc., Hauppauge, New York, 2000.

———. *The Everything Cat Book, 2nd Edition.* Adams Media, Massachusetts, 2007.

Whiteley, H. Ellen, D.V.M. *Understanding and Training Your Cat or Kitten.* Crown Trade Paperbacks, New York, 1994.

Magazines

Cat Fancy
P.O. Box 52864
Boulder, CO 80322-2864
(800)365-4421
www.catfancymagazine.com

I Love Cats
450 Seventh Ave., Suite 1701
New York, NY 10123
(212)244-2351
www.iluvcats.com

Answers to "Test Your Knowledge of Cats"

1. Yes, cats sleep up to 16 hours a day.
2. No, the urge to hunt is also dissipated through play.
3. No, sweets are unhealthy and chocolate is poisonous.
4. No, they usually make friends very quickly.
5. No, but it needs lots of activities.
6. Yes, the household must be cat-friendly.
7. Yes, but it is less obvious than the hierarchy among dogs.
8. Yes, often even before other symptoms present themselves.
9. No, there are also some real party poopers.
10. Yes, if you cleverly persuade them to cooperate.
11. No, in total darkness, cats are blind.

Photographers

Arco Images/De Meester; Artemis View/Elsner; Norvia Behling; Gerr Bucsis & Barbara Somerville; Cogis/Dufresne; Cogis/Gauzargue Cogis/Hermeline; Giel; Juniors/Born; Juniors/Kolmikow; Juniors Kuczka; Juniors/Schanz; Juniors/Wegler; Kuhn; M4GMBH/more4cats Pussy-Versand; Schanz; Steimer; Wegler; Zefaimages and Zefaimages Benser.

Acknowledgments

M4GMBH/more4cats, Neu-Ulm (cat nest bed, page 30) and Pussy-Versand, Wegberg (scratch board/fitness studio, page 22, thermal cush ion, snuggle sack, paradise of warmth, pages 30/31). The author and the publisher thank attorney Reinhard Hahn for his advice on lega matters.

English translation © Copyright 2007
by Barron's Educational Series, Inc.
Text © Copyright 2006 by Gräfe and Unzer Verlag
GmbH, Munich, Germany
The title of the German book is *300 Fragen zur Katze*

English version translated by Kathleen Luft
Additional text provided by Karen Davis

All inquiries should be addressed to:
Barron's Educational Series, Inc.
250 Wireless Boulevard
Hauppauge, NY 11788
www.barronseduc.com

Library of Congress Catalog Card No. 2006933269

ISBN-13: 978-0-7641-3739-6
ISBN-10: 0-7641-3739-5

Printed in China
9 8 7 6 5 4 3 2 1